Page and Stage

An Approach to Script Analysis

Stanley Vincent Longman

University of Georgia

PEARSON

Boston ■ New York ■ San Francisco
Mexico City ■ Montreal ■ Toronto ■ London ■ Madrid ■ Munich ■ Paris
Hong Kong ■ Singapore ■ Tokyo ■ Cape Town ■ Sydney

Series Editor: *Molly Taylor*
Editorial Assistant: *Michael Kish*
Marketing Manager: *Mandee Eckersley*
Production Administrator: *Anna Socrates*
Editorial-Production Service: *Omegatype Typography, Inc.*
Manufacturing Buyer: *JoAnne Sweeney*
Composition and Prepress Buyer: *Linda Cox*
Cover Administrator: *Kristina Mose-Libon*
Electronic Composition: *Omegatype Typography, Inc.*

For related titles and support materials, visit our online catalog at www.ablongman.com.

Between the time Website information is gathered and published, some sites may have closed. Also, the transcription of URLs can result in typographical errors. The publisher would appreciate notification where these errors occur so that they may be corrected in subsequent editions.

Library of Congress Cataloging-in-Publication Data

Longman, Stanley Vincent.
    Page and stage : an approach to script analysis / Stanley Vincent Longman.
        p.   cm.
    Includes bibliographical references and index.
    ISBN 0-205-37822-6 (alk. paper)
    1. Drama—Explication.   2. Drama—History and criticism—Theory, etc.   3.
Theater—Production and direction.   I. Title.

PN1707.L66 2004
808.2—dc21

                                                                                    2003049610

Printed in the United States of America

10 9 8 7 6 5 4 3 2 1   08 07 06 05 04 03

CONTENTS

APPENDICES

PREFACE

This book has been a long while in the making. It began over thirty years ago when Leighton Ballew, then Head of the Department of Drama and Theatre at the University of Georgia, assigned me to teach a class called "Play Analysis." I had not taught such a class before. At the same time I was engaged in directing several large-scale productions, for which I felt compelled to draft thorough analytical notes of the sort that could be useful to the designers with whom I collaborated as well as to myself prior to going into rehearsal. Out of these experiences I developed an approach to script analysis. It had to recognize the conditions under which plays operate on stage and especially the ways plays open themselves to audiences, who are the ultimate collaborators. It also had to be pragmatic. Unlike literary interpretation, script analysis has a very practical side. Anyone engaged in realizing a play on stage undertakes some form of analysis of the script, but many people do so only intuitively, almost denying they are really doing it at all. I considered it a valuable enterprise to set down an approach to analysis that could avoid problems, lead to more meaningful stagings, and yet also illuminate how plays work. This book is the result.

Acknowledgments

I am grateful to the many students who shared their insights as the course itself evolved. I would like to thank the reviewers of this book: Gayle Austin, Georgia State University; Kathleen Campbell, Austin College; and Robyn Quick, Towson University. I also am thankful to the many colleagues who have listened to my ideas, responded with their own, and encouraged a continual exploration of the subject. Among them I would number Leighton Ballew, Gerald Kahan, William Wolak, E. A. Peyroux, Joseph Stell, Oscar Brockett, Howard Stein, R. S. Crane, Jerry Crawford, Roland Reed, Ron Willis, Virginia Scott, Corinne Jacker, Frank Gagliano, Charles Eidsvik, August Staub, Douglas M. Young, Alessandro Marchetti, Luisella Sala, Luigi Allegri, Luigi Lunari, Les Wade, Peter Pauzé, and many, many others. It has been an exciting journey of discovery. To these people I add my wife, Ruth Farstrup Longman, whose encouragement kept me moving forward in this project and whose critical readings have been of enormous help.

INTRODUCTION

Page and Stage lays out a method for analyzing play scripts. Scripts are peculiar in that they are paradoxically both complete and unrealized. Inasmuch as they tell stories, create their own distinct fictional worlds, and develop identifiable characters, they are complete pieces of literature. They can be analyzed much as one would a short story or a novel. They are a form of fiction. At the same time, they are composed for the purpose of providing a basis for a play to take place on a stage before a gathered audience. Plays require planning, a requirement usually met by scripting. In this sense, scripts are unrealized plays. Any method for analyzing scripts must take this stage dimension into account. Playwrights write with a stage in mind, and we must read them with a "theatre in our head," to borrow a phrase from Kenneth Thorpe Rowe.

Because of these conditions, scripts operate in a context. What is on the page relates to what will be on the stage, and what is on stage relates to the audience gathered in the house, and the whole of the theatrical experience relates to the world beyond the confines of the theatre, to the human experience. No play works in a vacuum. It resonates and it does so deliberately.

Deliberately is a key word here. We might wonder how in the world we can analyze a script if we do not actually see it performed as a play on stage and bring to it that shared experience only an assembled crowd can have. Perhaps we can relish the script's allusions and parallels with our own experience, but a play is much more than a commentary on life. It has a vivid immediacy unlike anything that a short story, novel, or poem can create. That very immediacy is built into the script. Although we cannot directly experience the play with only the script in hand, we can find its sources and values. Unrealized as a play script must be, it still contains implicitly all those factors that will give life to the theatre experience of the eventual play. If this were not the case, no one could produce a play except by working from the ground up, improvising with the actors and engaging the immediate collaboration of designers. But people do produce plays from scripts. They do so by analyzing them. Whether or not they acknowledge it, every director, every actor, every designer analyzes scripts. This book can make that process more effective, more efficient, and more insightful.

This is not, however, simply a handbook for producing artists of the theatre. It should prove useful as well for anyone who must undertake the study of dramatic literature and theatre history, whether for academic or critical purposes. In short, any time a script is taken under examination, the reader must bring to it some sense of how the page relates to the stage and to the world beyond. The method explored here may open up facets inherent in the play script that might otherwise remain ignored. People often speak of plays that "do not read well, but play marvelously." The truth is that it is the reader who is not reading well.

Nor is this book intended as an exploration of dramatic theory. Many ideas have been put forth to provide a theoretical perspective on drama, never more than in the present age. In the last quarter of the twentieth century, theoretical discourse became increasingly intense. Generally, the effort is to place drama in some larger context of human experience such as the nature of the mind, overarching historical patterns, or forces of society. Out of this endeavor have come such schools of thought as archetypal criticism, Marxist criticism, the New Criticism, New Historicism, phenomenology, semiotics, reader response theory, deconstructionism, New Formalism, and others. Although these schools of thought provide fascinating and vigorously argued ideas, for the most part they serve to relate literature and drama to larger issues. Here we are interested in focusing on the process of analysis. Although we borrow ideas from some of these theories, especially from New Criticism and phenomology, the emphasis is on the pragmatic: How are plays put together and how is that evident in scripts?

Page and Stage is divided into three parts, beginning with an examination of the nature of the drama. Like any art form, the drama seeks to recast human experience in order to reflect on it. Recasting experience means first of all adopting a mode of expression. Experience can be recast in rhythms and tones (as in music), in line, color, and mass (as in graphic art), in the play of words (as in poetry), or in storytelling (as in narrative fiction). The dramatic mode consists of human experience manifested as spectacle. Part I is devoted to examining the dramatic mode: What is the essence of the dramatic? What is the relationship between drama and life? To answer these questions, we should arrive at a definition of a play, and we should then see how a play relates to playwright and to audience. The essence of the drama, and the basis for this approach to the process of analysis, lies in sharply drawn tensions that engage the audience and bind events into a coherent arc of action.

Part II deals with the stage medium. Just as every art form adopts a mode of expression, each one must resort to some medium. In the case of graphic art, the medium might be painting or etching or bas-relief sculpture. In the case of poetry, the medium consists of words on a page. In the case of drama, the medium is the stage populated by living and breathing performers. In the modern world, it might also consist of the screen, both big and silver and little and glowing varieties, or the radio speaker. Here we concentrate on the stage medium. Traditionally, scripts have been analyzed as they develop action in time moving through the phases of exposition, complication, crisis, climax, and resolution. Such an approach ignores the context in which a play operates. A play exists in both time and space. The stage is by definition a confined space of one sort or another. Drama happens in a place. How that space is defined and characterized has a tremendous impact on how the play itself works. Tensions can emerge from the way in which the stage space addresses the audience. Or they may emerge from juxtaposing one part of the stage with another or the whole of the stage with the fictional world beyond it, things that may be happening "out there." The context in which action takes place also draws on past events, on what has happened before our encounter with the world of the play. Moreover, the characters themselves may be set in some sort of opposition or contrast that establishes potential tensions among them. The stage itself assumes naturally a double existence as both stage and fictional world, and that too can be a source of tension. All of these are contextual matters.

Now, it is also true that a play exists in time. Plays, after all, occur. They happen, and when they cease happening, when the curtain comes down or the stage lights go out, the play evaporates, leaving behind only a memory. That is the ephemeral nature of dramatic art, but it is also the rationale behind a play's movement through time, the phases of dramatic action. Plays tend to move forward through shifting tensions that elaborate on some abiding, fundamental tension. This is what occasions both the rising action, culminating in a climactic moment when that fundamental tension snaps, and the falling action that brings the play to its end. Although the traditional phases can be useful, they need to be examined with an eye on the context in which they occur. After all, this is not just a matter of charting the play's action in terms of the events that occur within its plot. It is also a matter of placing the events, or changes, in the surrounding context What constitutes an "event" may not be simply a matter of a new direction in plot. It may derive from many factors both within and without the fictional world of the play. Events, in other words, are not tied exclusively to plot or story line. Anton Chekhov's *The Three Sisters* or Samuel Beckett's *Waiting for Godot* or David Mamet's *American Buffalo* are all three full of events, but their stories are scarcely tellable. To get at this, it is valuable to break down the action into its component segments, each based on the development of a tension. This section on the temporal dimension of drama develops a way of segmenting action meaningfully.

In Part III, questions of form, style, and meaning come under examination. Inasmuch as drama is the product of a vision of reality, much of what a play "means" comes not so much from what "happens" as from how we are made to experience what happens. Style and form are equally important in this regard. An event rendered in one style and granted shape under one form may be flat and meaningless, but rendered in another style or form it may take on rich significance. These chapters explore the distinction between form and style and the relationship between the two. In a sense, the issue comes back to the all-important nature of the audience's involvement in the drama. Without the audience, plays are flat and empty, as anyone knows who has been through the final polishing phase of a well-rehearsed play. An audience joins in the play by its recognition and acceptance of the play's vision. Plays by their very nature incorporate their audiences. How they do so is crucial to script analysis. We have to go beyond isolating major dramatic questions, expositions, complications, and climaxes. Dramatic structure exists for the purpose of engaging audiences and addressing issues beyond the immediate boundaries of the stage or the theatre. Although one may isolate some structural elements that plays all tend to share, each play is its own unique experience, using the stage its own way, eliciting very particular responses from its audience, and providing its own vision of reality.

Now, one might argue that a play always means something different to one person than it does to the next, even witnesses of the same performance. Naturally, there is some truth to this. Plays are subjective experiences and they seek to move us, to affect us. Reaching out beyond itself, a play will touch on one person's experience in a way not shared with another. Nevertheless, plays are not illogical, motley collections of unrelated images, events, and spectacles—not even the most postmodern of plays. Postmodern plays such as Heiner Müller's *Hamletmachine* or Robert Wilson's *the CIVIL warS* do deliberately splinter effects so as to engage one portion of the audience in a way distinct from another part of the audience. But even these plays possess an internal design. Given a disciplined subjectivity, we can get at the factors that contribute to the play's effects. The method described here entails that very sort of discipline. It is ultimately pragmatic in the best and richest sense of that word. The method explores what *works* in a play. Ideas about a play have greater or lesser value depending on how well they illuminate the play as a whole. The idea, for example, that Hamlet suffers from an Oedipus complex and is fatally in love with his mother is an intriguing idea, but it is also one that opens up very little about *The Tragedy of Hamlet, Prince of Denmark* as a whole. It gives an interesting slant to the bedchamber scene in which Hamlet confronts Gertrude. But the play's action develops on so many other levels. The uncertainty about the validity of the Ghost and the insidious court politics that have deprived Hamlet of his succession to the throne and now threaten his own well-being, if not his life, are factors much more pertinent to the overall action of the play. They are ones that necessitate hiding his true feelings and intentions. They are enough to account for his assuming his "antic disposition." He must be constantly performing a role for the court, and, to force King Claudius to perform an "honest" role, he has the players perform a play much like the murder of the previous king, Hamlet's father. *Hamlet* deals with playacting itself on multiple levels. This too is an intriguing view of the play's action, but it also illuminates far more of the play's total experience. Analysis should put the parts of a play in perspective by showing their relationship to the whole.

The last chapter in the book builds on the principles that have been developed and presents a process for script analysis, outlining that process step by step. If the parts need to be examined in relation to the whole, these steps have to isolate the significant parts, recognizing how they develop and contribute to the play's overall experience. The important premise for the process is the recognition that the parts develop through time. A play is composed of moments that emerge out of the manipulation of the stage medium. So the process is based on a "vertical" analysis of the script, examining how the medium is used moment by moment, as opposed to a "horizontal" one following the medium's elements (plot, character, theme, dialogue, spectacle, for example) one by one through the duration of the play. One moment may depend on one set of stage elements, the next on quite another set. The audience, after all, experiences the play that way. Analyses of three very distinct scripts appear as appendices at the end of this book to illustrate this vertical approach. This last chapter also includes descriptions of the special considerations that govern the work of theatrical artists—directors, actors, and designers—undertaking the process of making a script into a performance as a play. The approach described in this book should prove generally useful in the production process, but that process entails some special concerns that can translate into visual terms and into performance.

Treating the script in pragmatic terms as a document related to performance should provide not only practical steps in the production process but also valuable insights into the values and effects central to the play's ultimate experience. It is in this hope that the book is prepared. It ought then to have use for script interpretation as well as for play production.

1 The Nature of Drama: What Is a Play?

"I read a play last night." This is a statement you might well have heard or said yourself. Technically, it is an impossibility. A play is a performance presented to an audience. You cannot read a performance. You have to attend a performance. In fact, plays are constructed, rehearsed, planned, and prepared specifically for a gathered audience. They are not meant to be read. As a convenience, however, plays usually are scripted. A script is a useful device in the preparation of a play. To put on a play requires some sort of plan. Even one presented improvisationally, as many contemporary performance art pieces are and the commedia dell'arte always was, requires some sort of blueprint for the action. That blueprint may not contain all the words to be spoken or describe all the physical activities to accompany them, but it does provide an outline of the experience the play is to present. It is a script. And one can read a script.

Reading a play script is generally not quite as easy as reading a short story or a novel. The reason is that a novel is complete. It is all there, and you experience it on the terms the novelist intended you to experience it. A playwright, however, puts words on paper with an eye to what will eventually happen on stage. The playwright intends for you to experience the play there, not on the page. Many factors have to be shaped and controlled beyond the words that appear immediately before your eyes on the page. It is enlightening on this score to recognize the peculiar nature of the word for the person who deals with all these factors of composing a script: the playwright. The word is not *playwrite* or *playwriter.* The "wright" portion of the word is revealing. It is a slightly archaic word that refers to a person who builds or constructs something. We use it to refer to people who build ships, wheels, *and* plays: shipwrights, wheelwrights, and playwrights. In other words, the act of putting together a play script is not just a matter of writing down some dialogue. It calls for building a set of actions bound together in a way that can sustain an audience's involvement from curtain up to curtain down. This fact is reflected in many other words we use in reference to plays: *dramatic structure, dramaturgy, scenario, acts* and *scenes, speeches,* and *stage directions.*

All this has important implications for those of us engaged in analyzing scripts. If the playwright is building something, we have to find a way to perceive that structure. What exactly is a playwright manipulating if not words on a page? What is a play anyway? One could describe a play as an energy system. The energy comes out of a fundamental but constantly shifting set of tensions, and it manifests itself in action. These lines of tension require close shaping in order to be perceptible to the audience, and they bind together the experience. That is only a beginning. We need first of all to consider in much more detail what exactly a play is. In order to arrive at a satisfactory definition, however, we should put plays in context. They are a form of dramatic art: What is the nature of the dramatic? In what sense is drama an art?

The Art of Dramatic Art

The term "art" conjures up a vision of some exalted and rarefied offering intended for a connoisseur or a coterie of knowledgeable viewers. Only the initiated have access to it. The same goes for "the Theatre." Very special, mysterious, profound things happen in the Theatre. Very Special People go to the Theatre. The fact is that there is nothing inherently exalted about Art. In the strictest and simplest sense, art is simply the product of a certain kind of human endeavor. It is a category of activity.

At one time, the term referred to a craft, a set of skills necessary for the production of some commodity. We still use the term that way in describing, for example, the art of shipbuilding or the art of making wheels. In the eighteenth century, people began to make a distinction between "fine" art and "useful" art. Some art is applied, they recognized, to the construction of practical objects such as furniture, utensils, carriages, and so forth, whereas other forms of art are "fine" in the sense that they justify themselves through the attractiveness and elegance of their products. A piece of fine art is simply a pleasure to behold. Paintings, symphonies, poems, statues, novels, and plays are of this sort. The term aesthetic applies to the experience of fine art because it refers to the sensitive perception of created beauty. It is the opposite, in a way, of "anesthetic," which of course means a lack of sensitivity. When we witness an artwork, we have a heightened sense of our own life.

Narrowed down in this way, how might we define "art"? Art is a recasting of experience in a distinct medium of expression. The artist manipulates the material of a medium (such as pigments on canvas, tones sounded in rhythm, words on a page, carved stone, and so forth) to provide a spectator, audience, or reader with a reflection of the experience of being human. That reflection is itself an experience, rendered enjoyable in some way or in some spirit. To call something a "work of art" is merely to recognize that someone has manipulated the materials for the primary purpose of affecting other people. The work could be an opera or a rock concert, a marble statue or a piece of whittled wood, a five-act tragedy or a stand-up comedy routine, a painting or a comic strip. All of these are works of art.

Indeed, analyzing the comic strip may be a good way of seeing the essential elements of an art. With it, we can avoid the exalted, rarefied, and slightly mystical qualities people tend to associate with art, for the comic strip is an art form that we witness in our daily lives. We accept it readily as a distinct form that does not have to be exactly like life in order to reflect on life. We do not question its right to occupy its own ground, shape its characters in black ink outlines, and use balloons for speeches and frames for segments of action.

The comic strip in Figure 1.1 is a piece of art about a piece of art. Calvin explains to Hobbes his avant-garde snow sculpture. The snowman is "secretly

FIGURE 1.1

ironic" but will appeal to the tastes of the common public. Calvin has chosen this way to play on aesthetic response. The comic strip itself, of course, is a work of art. We relish it as a reflection on certain "artistic" attitudes encountered in our own society. Here a boy talks to his stuffed tiger about his artistic endeavors and we chuckle. Meanwhile, the comic strip artist, Bill Watterson, has manipulated the material of his medium to conduct us into the experience of Calvin and Hobbes. First of all, we are to accept the line drawings as standing for a reality that is not actually present: a living stuffed tiger, a snowman, and a boy in the snow. Then we take the words written above their heads and circled with a point directed at the speaker to be dialogue exchanged between tiger and boy. Moreover, the four squares move us through time as if the characters were really engaged in activity despite their being "frozen" in blocks of time. These are all **conventions** on which comic strips rely. Every art form requires conventions; they are agreements with the viewer to accept one thing for another. Beyond the standard conventions, the artist here also creates a special convention: We are to accept a stuffed animal as the real tiger friend that Calvin imagines him to be. So we not only take the line drawings, frames, and balloons to stand for something else, but we also take Calvin's view of reality and accept the stuffed animal as a tiger.

This example illustrates the four basic characteristics of art:

1. It is not life, yet, like life, it is an experience.
2. It deliberately sets itself apart from life.
3. It operates on its own terms, with its own materials, within its own bounds.
4. It seeks to reflect life: It is about being human.

Each of these characteristics deserves a brief explanation. First, the artist does not seek to duplicate life. Life can take care of itself. Nevertheless, the artist is interested in giving the viewer an experience that in some way heightens awareness of life. On this score, it is very different from intellectual activity that attempts one way or another to distill and explain the phenomena of experience in rational terms. The philosopher or the historian will express ideas in the form of an essay, which is not a work of art except insofar as it may be elegant, eloquent, and pleasurable to read. These are by-products of the effort to communicate ideas. A work of art, by contrast, gives us an experience that affects us, and that is the chief aim of the artist.

Second, a work of art is always removed from the immediate domain of everyday life. If art is not life, it nevertheless is about life. For that to happen, it has to separate itself from the actual. Every art form uses devices created to enhance that separation. Paintings, for example, are normally encased in frames, which tell us not to confuse the artwork with the wall. Statues are stood on pedestals to avoid confusion with ordinary furniture. Novels consist of words on pages bound together within the covers of books. Plays depend on the proscenium arch, the arena, or pools of light. Although it is true that some experimental theatre, such as "happenings" and environmental performances, seek to blur this separation, they nevertheless create spectacles that immediately detach themselves from the surroundings.

Third, a piece of art not only operates within its own bounds apart from the life around it, but it also uses the specific materials of a medium of expression. The artwork might be stone carved to create an experience, or notes sounded by passing a bow over the strings of a violin, or lines on paper created by pen and ink. Moreover, these materials naturally limit the experience any one medium is capable of conveying, but this limitation also means that the artist is free to establish the distinct terms on which the art operates. These are the conventions described earlier.

Finally, the experience created distinct from the everyday serves to reflect on human experience. We who are in the midst of living have scarcely the time or the perspective to sense what life is all about. Art gives us a chance to see life being lived and sense its value and meaning. In other words, the work of art separates itself from life in order to reflect on life.

This description of art is as true of a play as of any other artwork. The dramatist first separates an experience from its actual context in life and then recasts it in the medium of the stage or the screen. In the audience, we become engaged, even enthralled, with this new experience in proportion to the opportunity it affords us to reflect on life itself. A truly powerful play causes us to see ourselves as we have never quite done before and with a leisure life itself rarely allows us.

The Dramatic in Dramatic Art

Drama shares all these characteristics with other arts. It also shares another quality. Like all the arts, the drama is an outgrowth of a basic instinct in the human spirit. There is a natural impulse to dance, to paint, to make music—*and* to perform roles. There have been periods in history when theatre was outlawed or its activity severely proscribed. Even under those conditions, people found ways to perform for other people. Despite many soundings of the alarm that the theatre is dying— and we hear them even today—it never does. The act of presenting oneself to other people is the fundamental act of theatre. It is also a fundamental human impulse.

Consider the number of times in the course of a single day you find yourself confronting other people. Whenever we encounter others, we are always in some measure aware of the act of presenting ourselves and almost as often conscious of the effect we are having (or wish we were having). This everyday experience contains the essence of the dramatic: the **encounter.** It occurs when we encounter one another to make up an audience that then encounters performers presenting spectacles of their encounters as characters. They may be encountering one another, their fates, some absurd circumstance, their past lives, or their inner fears. Any of these can provide the stuff of drama. The encounter is drama's basic motif. Encounters in real life, however, have varying degrees of effect on those who participate in them. The more striking or profound the effect, the more likely we are to call it dramatic.

It can be useful to examine instances in real life that produce dramatic effect. Some events, by their very nature, spellbind the onlooker. Without any contriving, a palpable tension causes onlookers or participants to sit up and take notice. A man standing on a window ledge twenty stories above the street is dramatic in this sense. Assuming that he is genuinely committed to suicide, his purpose has nothing to do with affecting the casual passerby. On the other hand, he may wish to create guilt or compassion in the person who pushed him to this extreme, and in that case he is "being dramatic." He has chosen this graphic expression of his despair and disappointment. He is making a public display of it. In short, he is making theatre.

One reason that professional press photography and television video or sound bites can be so powerful is their capacity to isolate a highly expressive moment in the lives, joys, or sorrows of other people. Each of us has a gallery of these images in the memory, even if some of them occurred before our time: soldiers raising the American flag on Iwo Jima, General MacArthur wading ashore in the Philippines, the returning sailor bending his girlfriend double in a homecoming kiss on V-J Day, Jack Ruby shooting Lee Harvey Oswald, Neil Armstrong's first step on the moon, the burning naked little girl in Vietnam, Nixon wagging two fingers of each hand at the door of his airplane, the man standing squarely in front of a military tank in Tiananmen Square in Beijing, the half naked corpse of an American serviceman dragged through the streets of Mogodishu, a weeping Tonya Harding showing the judges her ill-fitting skate, the slow chase of O. J. Simpson's Ford Bronco, the parade of the starving and homeless making their way out of Rwanda, the expressionless face of Osama bin Laden, jet airliners crashing into the towers of the World Trade Center, and so forth. All of these are powerful images that have caught the emotion of a decisive moment. These are intense encounters, instances of the dramatic.

Occasionally—and this includes some of the instances just listed—someone will make a deliberate effort to work an effect. Social or political protest, of the sort the United States, France, and other countries witnessed in the late sixties and early seventies, often took on dramatic qualities. Protestors organized and manipulated events to affect others. The Catonsville Nine carried files from the offices of a draft board to the street, where they poured blood on them. The spectacle was hard to ignore. Those were times of "consciousness raising"—a phrase that, however cumbersome, holds rich dramatic connotation. Such contrivance does not belong to protestors alone; those in power also resort to the dramatic. Public appearances of leading figures are often elaborately planned affairs, calculated to make a leader appear larger than life, a person of formidable dimensions. Nowadays, no powerful figure can do without public relations experts who know how to manipulate moments for the greatest positive impact.

None of this is meant to imply that the dramatic is inherently false or gimmicky. It is, however, inherently sensational in the sense that it relies on spectacle that makes a direct appeal to our senses. Of course, the spectacle can be presented for good or for ill. No event is really dramatic unless it is "played" to a gathered audience. There is an old philosophical conundrum: When a tree falls in the forest and no one is there, does it make a sound? Likewise, when someone puts on a play and no one is there, is it a play? The answer in this instance is clear—no. All the drama evaporates if the suicide ledge is above an empty street or if no one is out in front of the draft board offices when the blood is poured. The same is true of a play. If no one is "out front," there is no drama. Naturally, everyone involved in the creation of a play is intensely interested in the crowd out front. Every task—writing the play, planning the production, rehearsing the actors—contributes to producing an effect on an audience. Although the best effects are those the audience feels happen spontaneously, without contrivance, such effects require the most work. They also require that someone *be* out front.

The dramatic, then, is a part of life; we see it daily. We encounter it when we meet a friend, when we witness a planned event, or when we suddenly come upon an intriguing act. Naturally, we look for it when we go to the theatre and we are disappointed if it is not there. It occurs whenever a person engages in the act of presenting himself or herself to other people, and it entails the motif of encounter, multiplied on many levels. This is what we might call the "dramatic mode," which has five distinguishing elements:

1. The first and most basic ingredient in the dramatic mode is the **encounter.** It occurs on the most fundamental level when spectator meets spectacle. This moment produces an immediate polarity, a palpable tension, which prompts the spectator to watch, to listen, and to attend the event. The dramatist seeks to play on this tension, to create and sustain effects and responses.

2. **Polarity and tension** provide the fundamental dramatic devices. Any onlooker becomes more or less involved in proportion to how much seems to be at stake. Tension may take multiple forms: conflict, incongruity, irony, disparity, contrast, anticipation. A play is an energy system of lines of tension; the basic tension inherent in the act of encounter is multiplied in a myriad ways.

3. The dramatic mode depends on **action,** action that we can directly see and hear. Drama occurs. When it ceases to occur, it ceases to exist. In this respect, drama is perhaps more lifelike than any other art form. Life too ceases to exist when it ceases to happen. It cannot be encapsulated, contained, or frozen without destroying it. Moreover, one senses drama in much the same way one senses life: by observing the actions of others. Just as we come to know other people by seeing them and hearing them, so we become involved in a play and its characters. The objective experience of our eyes and ears lets us translate action into inner life.

4. The dramatic mode depends on a **sense of immediacy;** it appears to be happening *now.* This is the source of the old adage that "the theatre dies every night when the curtain goes down." Dramatic action resides in what Thornton Wilder has called a "perpetual present time." A novel, on the other hand, is a story that appears over and done with. A play carries with it the illusion of the first time, the sense that it is occurring now, before our eyes, spontaneously, without plan or contrivance. Paradoxically, only careful planning and contrivance—and continual repetition and practice—can produce this illusion.

5. As a result of all these conditions, the dramatic mode employs a **driving force,** an impetus that moves action forward against odds of some sort. The spirit of encounter, the use of poles of tension, the reliance on action, and the sense of immediacy all play into the emergence of a driving force. Typically, what keeps a spectator's attention is the sense of something pending, something about to happen, something acting against resistance, all in the immediate present.

Mode versus Medium

Thus far the dramatic mode has been described without regard to the medium in which it appears. "Mode" is significantly different from "medium." Mode refers to a manner or manifestation of experience. The dramatic mode is experience manifested through the spectacle of human action. Other modes besides the dramatic include the musical mode, employing tone and rhythm; the graphic mode, using line, color, or mass in two-dimensional space; the lyrical mode, using the play of words; the narrative mode, using words for storytelling. Medium refers to the context, conditions, and materials of an art form in which experience is recreated. Thus painting is a medium using pigments applied to a two-dimensional surface. The cartoon and the comic strip use ink drawn on paper, but they tap the graphic mode as much as painting does. Some experiences lend themselves to re-creation better in one medium than another. The glory of a stupendous sunset, for example, can be caught in painting but would be difficult in a cartoon and virtually impossible in bas-relief sculpture.

Through the ages, the dramatic mode has found its medium in the theatre, in the actual encounter of performers and spectators. Our age has produced new media, each of which provides a home for the dramatic: radio, television, and cinema. All of these—the stage, the speaker box, the tube, and the silver screen—have the capacity to present the spectacle of human life through action, and this of course is the dramatic mode. Just as in the contrast between the painting, cartoon, and bas-relief sculpture, all of which are visual media, one dramatic medium may reflect a certain human experience more vividly than another. A movie, for example, can convincingly portray the agony of loneliness through the interplay of images, but a stage play attempting the same thing would produce unendurable tedium.

What differentiates the dramatic media is the essential material they employ. In the confined space of the stage, performers present themselves to a gathered audience. Television and cinema present the interplay of moving images on a two-dimensional screen. Radio presents suggestive sound. These media may all serve purposes other than dramatic ones. The stage could be the arena for acrobatic tricks, magic acts, or dances. Film can be used for recording actual events as documentaries or for rendering visual designs in motion (what some call "pure cinema"). Television can be used for journalistic reporting, game shows, sports, or advertisements, and indeed these take up the majority of program time. When, however, these media use the images or sounds of performers to create a spectacle of imagined human action, they become dramatic. It is this ingredient of *imagined* human action that makes the difference. Whenever imagined activity accompanies the actual presentation of performances, images, or sounds, the magic of drama can emerge.

Watching a play, we translate what we actually see into an imagined life that is not really there. We observe a succession of moving images passing across a movie screen (perhaps the image of a coffin being lowered into a grave followed by one of an eye shedding a tear) and create in our minds an imagined experience that was never really there at all (death and grief). On stage a Shakespearean soliloquy presents us with an actor speaking alone, and we translate this activity into a character ruminating in his mind. There is always a degree of disparity between the actual experience of the stage or screen and the imagined experience it summons up. Living actors performing before us on stage create characters living their lives in our imagination. Characters exist only in our minds as products of the signals provided by actors before us. In this sense, no matter what the medium, the dramatic is always double-edged; the actual and the imagined exist side by side.

This book concentrates on the stage medium. Partly this is because the demand for us to develop an approach to play scripts intended for the stage is far greater than that for screenplays. By and large, movies are experienced as produced plays and relatively rarely read as scripts. Anyone involved in stage production, whether in the capacity of director, designer, or actor, will almost always have to deal with a script. Nevertheless, many of the principles and methods explored here may be applied to screen drama as well.

The Double Edge of Drama:
Actual Performance versus Pretense

For the audience, drama entails two experiences coinciding in time. We simultaneously encounter actual performers moving in the actual space of the stage and characters living their lives in some virtual world of their own. This double edge to the drama is part of what gives it its appeal and fascination. There is a natural playfulness inherent in plays, a kind of childlike charm. When we go to the theatre, we engage our imagination with the performers, and together we create in our minds a rich and full world that is literally not there. You cannot go to the theatre and actually meet Hamlet. You can go to the theatre and witness this or that actor playing the role and together with him create Hamlet in your "mind's eye." This experience involves a delicious tension that Gary Schmidgall calls "the Gemini effect."

We are simultaneously enjoying the performance of the actor and experiencing vicariously the life of the character. We relish both and let them exist together in a kind of mutual suspension.

The dramatic mode entails that wonderfully ironic experience Samuel Johnson called the "willing suspension of disbelief," later fully described by Samuel Coleridge. It is a calculated phrase. We do not literally believe the illusion of characters living their lives before our eyes, but we do, for the time being, agree to suspend our disbelief—agree, that is, to accept the illusion for the sake of whatever it may show us about human reality. We know full well that we are witnessing events on a stage over a span of time, say from eight until ten in the evening, but we are also willing to believe that much more time has elapsed and that the stage is also somewhere else, perhaps far removed from where we presently sit. The opening scene of *Hamlet* illustrates this well. For the duration of the scene—some 175 lines (about twenty minutes' playing time)—we are on the ramparts of the castle at Elsinore from midnight until the cock's crow at dawn. Nights in Denmark may be short, but not that short. For the sake of the illusion and the play as a whole, we accept passing the night in Denmark.

This state of mind, this childlike charm, is essential to the experience of theatre. If you lose it, you also lose the capacity to involve yourself in the dramatic action of a play. This mind-set derives from the contrary pulls of two mental impulses: **empathy** and **aesthetic distance.** Empathy pulls you into the world of the play. In the throes of empathy, you vicariously undergo some of the same emotions the characters feel. This emotion is a stronger version of the more common sympathy. The prefix *sym* means "with" and *pathy* means "feeling." To sympathize means to feel with someone, to recognize another's emotion and take pity. *Em* means "into," so empathizing is a case of entering into another person's frame of mind, feeling the same emotion, as if you were yourself caught in that person's life.

Aesthetic distance pulls you out of the play, recognizing it as a product of artistic endeavor. To use Oscar Brockett's terminology, it is "a state of detached contemplation" of the play as a contrivance, a work of art. In this spirit, we may take pleasure in the choices an actor makes, in the arrangement of events the playwright has assembled, in the beauty of the stage lighting or the stage pictures created by the scenery and the direction. We may catch allusions and savor symbolic meanings. We expect the play to round out and conclude, leaving us with a final clinching impression.

Both of these mental impulses are at work simultaneously during the course of watching a play. At one moment, we may find ourselves admiring the way an effect was created and at another, feeling the intense emotion of a character. Ultimately, however, for willing suspension of disbelief to work, the two must be in balance. Aesthetic distance should balance out empathy. We might visualize the relationship in terms of a teeter-totter, with aesthetic distance at one end, empathy at the other, and willing suspension of disbelief as the fulcrum, as illustrated in Figure 1.2. It is quite possible for the enjoyment of a play to be spoiled when imbalance creeps in. If we witness actors who are not concentrating but rather glancing about the auditorium, perhaps even waving at friends they recognize, we are reminded at once that this is a contrivance and thus no empathy is possible. A pretentious

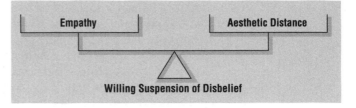

FIGURE 1.2   The teeter-totter model of the willing suspension of disbelief.

play that keeps reminding us what it means through heavy-handed symbolism destroys empathy. It is also possible for a play to overbalance in favor of empathy. The play calls on us to shed tears, and only later do we realize there was no substance to the matter. Soap operas, even really successful ones, deliberately try to maintain the illusion of an ongoing life, episode after episode, playing heavily on empathy. By having virtually no beginning or end, they seem to go on like life itself, day after day. This overbalance of empathy has led some disturbed people to assault actresses on the street because these fans perceive only the villainesses these actresses play on daytime television.

For the purposes of analysis, perhaps the most intriguing and revealing aspect of this balancing act lies in the way it offers a source of tension that the play can tap for its ongoing action. The mutual existence of actual activity and imagined activity can provide the audience with a crosscurrent of energy that can be very engaging. Actors may be doing one thing on stage while we are imagining the characters doing something quite different. The previous example of the Shakespearean soliloquy illustrates this possible tension: An actor stands on stage and talks while we imagine a character wrestling within his mind. Much more will be said later about this valuable source of tension.

A Play Finally Defined

Many definitions of a play have developed from ancient times to the present. None of them is definitive, so precise and accurate that we need search no further. The reason is that plays are ephemeral and ever changing, and they are by nature highly subjective. On the other hand, some of the definitions put forth in the past are revealing in some way. We might, at any rate, examine three of them.

Bernard Beckerman, in *The Dynamics of the Drama,* has provided us with a double definition, one for theatre and the other for drama. He points out that a definition would have to avoid the use of the verb "to be" because theatre and drama exist only when they are happening. We cannot say, "Theatre is" or "Drama is" this or that. We have to say, "Theatre occurs when . . . " He then provides this definition of theatre: "Theatre occurs when one or more persons, isolated in time and space, present themselves to others." At first sight, this would seem a sweeping definition. It would include a wide variety of activities, not just those we normally associate with the term "theatre," but also high-wire acts, magician's performances, speech making, boxing matches, and football games. Implicit in this definition, however, is some limiting of the scope. It implies that the act of self-presentation is central to theatre. In the case of the boxing match or the football game, self-presentation is secondary. The main purpose in football, for example, is to get the ball across the goal line more often than the opponents do. Inasmuch as this activity creates a spectacle that people will pay to see, an element of the theatrical is surely present, but it is not the main function of the football game. In the case of speech making, the act of self-presentation is crucial but not central: The main function is communication and sometimes persuasion. The other implication is that the self-presentation is done for the purpose of affecting others. The high-wire act, then, is truly an example of theatre. It consists plainly enough of a performer, isolated in time and space, presenting himself to others. No one in his right mind would do such a thing except to affect others or to prepare to affect others. That is the main function of theater. In short, whenever one sets aside a span of time and a performance space and then uses both for the act of self-presentation, one is indulging in theatre. It is a medium of expression, as discussed earlier, that consists of three-dimensional space occupied by living, breathing human beings presenting their very persons to other people gathered to watch. Theatre is fundamentally a spectacle—and that, of course, requires a spectator.

Beckerman goes on to define drama as a subcategory of theatre; it is theatre used for a more specific purpose. "Drama," he says, "occurs when one or more persons, isolated in time and space, present themselves in imagined acts to others." The addition of the phrase "in imagined acts" gives drama the capacity to deal with a fictional or virtual life. This is that double edge of drama described earlier. Where there are actors on stage, there are also characters in their world. The contrast, for example, between a high-wire acrobat and Marcel Marceau pantomiming a high-wire act illustrates vividly the difference between a theatrical performance and one that is also dramatic. The high-wire acrobat, isolated in time and space, creates sensations in the audience, expressed by appropriate oohs and aahs, by challenging actual danger, doing somersaults, flips, and twists on a tight wire high above the ground. The performance is all the more sensational if there is no net below. Marceau, on the other hand, performs his high-wire act on level ground. He faces no actual danger. Through his pantomime, we join in imagining him scaling a rope ladder, steadying himself on the wobbly platform, stepping gingerly out onto the high wire, and walking across it to the opposing platform. None of those things (ladder, platforms, or high wire) are physically there. Our focus of attention shifts from acrobatic challenges to gravity to the experience of the performer. Our empathy is engaged, and we sense the pain and agony of a performer who hates being "up there." That is now drama. It is a little play.

These definitions have the value of reminding us that plays require the medium of theatre, a space occupied by performers presenting themselves to others. Play scripts may be a form of literature, but they require a medium very different from any other form of literature. They have to make their way off the page and onto the stage. We also are reminded of the double edge of drama, for plays are both actual performance and virtual existence simultaneously. Isolation in time and space is also a factor of some importance. From the restricted time and space come sources of tension that can have meaningful value in the virtual world of a play. Times past and future can be set against the immediate present. Moreover, what is happening here may be contrasted to what is happening there, beyond the isolated space. Again, more will be said on these tensions later.

Going back more than a century earlier, is another revealing definition of the drama, this one in an essay titled "The Law of the Drama" written by French critic and theorist Ferdinand Brunetière in the 1860s. That was a time of positivism when people were convinced that a scientific, objective examination of any phenomenon would yield definitive insights. Brunetière called a play "a spectacle of a will striving toward a goal and conscious of the means it employs." The "law" of the title declared that the essence of the drama lay in strife—in struggle, conflict, and energy coupled with an aim or purpose. Thus, will, strife, and goal become central to the drama in Brunetière's view. This definition contains some useful observations. One is that a play consists of a spectacle; it appeals to our senses of sight and sound. Perhaps more important is the emphasis implicit here on action. Brunetière insists that a play requires conflict and that in turn requires a protagonist to embody the will and preferably an antagonist to provide the conflict. This may be rather too narrow a definition, but it is certainly true that the forward motion of a play derives from action.

Here, a worthwhile distinction should be drawn between "activity" and "action." If we isolate a performer in time and space, we naturally expect activity to help create spectacle. The performer must move about. If we are dealing with acrobatics, that may be enough, but once we have introduced "imagined acts," activity is not sufficient. In fact, aimless activity can quickly become tedious. Two characters seated and unmoving can speak such daggers that their exchange becomes spellbinding. We may witness them so alter their relationship that neither character can be the same again. A well-chosen word can have many times the force of a slap in the face. Activity becomes action whenever forces that seek to alter, confront, avoid, or adapt engage our attention and contribute to an altered world for the characters. Aristotle, writing in the fourth century B.C., declared plot to be the soul of the drama. What he meant was that organized action binds a play together. Just as action organizes activity, so plot organizes actions. As moment builds upon moment, a play develops a vector, a sense of anticipation and movement, that leads to an overarching action for the play as a whole. This is plot. Typically, a play begins when its world is somehow thrown off balance and ends when it finds a new balance. In between, the seeking of balance, that "striving will," produces the fundamental action, the plot of the play.

One other implication of Brunetière's definition deserves attention: his insistence on the will being "conscious of the means it employs." He does not insist that the will be fully aware of the goal, only of the means. The reason for this is probably that drama is conducted before our eyes and for our ears. Plays are objective in that sense. Because drama relies on observation, it requires that the will and its obstacles or contrary wills be observable. What we gather about the virtual world of the play and its characters we gather by what we see and hear the actors do and say. This in turn means that the characters must indulge in activities that we can read as actions. It means they must know *what* they are doing, even if they are not altogether positive about *why* they are doing it. Hamlet is a case in point: He is always active, always doing something, but not always quite sure what his goal is.

Now for one last definition, one that sums up what we have explored thus far. We have observed that art is a recasting of human experience in a distinct medium of expression. As an art, then, drama is a recasting of human experience in the form of a spectacle of life conducted through action based on pretense. Working backward through this statement, we find several key words. *Pretense* refers to the play's engagement of the audience's imagination to create a virtual world existing side by side with actual performance. It is that double edge of drama expressed in the phrase "willing suspension of disbelief." *Action* throws emphasis on the spectacle of a driving force, a will, seeking to alter and change the virtual world of the characters. Finally, *spectacle* alerts us to the fact that drama relies on the act of presentation. It is meant to be witnessed.

Tension as the Essence of the Dramatic

The first two fundamental questions to be asked about a play are "How is this play different from actuality?" and "Why is it different in that way?" We have already covered enough ground to recognize that plays are different from actuality. In fact, they are *deliberately* different. They set themselves apart from life, they recast human experience, and they use pretense and charted action. They are not life. This fact sometimes poses a problem, especially with "realistic" plays. These, of course, are plays that try to give an accurate picture of the way things really look and the way certain people really behave. Drama has naturally a very lifelike quality, consisting as it does of real people moving, acting, and reacting among themselves. We do not have such a problem with more abstract arts such as music or architecture. As Stark Young once pointed out, we do not criticize buildings for not looking more like trees, or Bach's *Coffee Cantata* for not sounding like coffee. We do, however, hear such remarks as "That was a wonderful play—that woman was just like my mother!" The point is that those people who are moving, acting, and reacting among themselves are also doing so in front of other people, the audience. So, even if they give the appearance of living a "real life," they are still immersed in the act of self-presentation. Their effort is to engage our interest and focus our attention. They do that by following certain lines of tension, embedded in the script, pertinent to the play's overall effect. It is these lines of tension that make a play different from actuality. The term "actuality" here refers to the physical phenomena of our day-to-day existence. Drama makes use of actuality in the form of living, breathing human beings moving in space before an audience. The audience in turn creates in its collective imagination a virtual existence of characters, and that virtual existence can then reflect reality through its sense of meaning or significance.

Brunetière suggested that plays are different from actuality by virtue of their essential ingredient: conflict. As he saw it, a play is always a spectacle of a will, embodied in the central character, the protagonist, striving through conflict with other characters, particularly the antagonist, until he or she finally reaches the goal or fails in the effort. This situation provides the design for dramatic structure. If we are to analyze a play, we must isolate the central conflict, identify the protagonist, and follow the rising action from the inciting incident through all manner of complications until the decisive climax moment opens up the resolution of the conflict and ends the play. This is traditional script analysis.

The difficulty here is that such an approach treats the play as a self-contained world, ignoring the context in which a play functions, a context that is shaped partly by the way in which it defines its space (and the space beyond the stage), its time (and all previous or future time), and especially its audience. The audience after all can be a source of energy in a play, and most often is. The result is that analysis reduces a play to its internal design, ignoring many other factors. It also treats the play as if it existed only as a temporal progression. This is more or less the case if we are only reading the script, but once it is a play on stage, its use of the stage space is a powerful factor shaping the audience's perception throughout the action.

A second problem is that not all plays are structured around conflict conducted by a clearly defined protagonist. Many plays not based on conflict nevertheless hold audiences in rapt attention. Anton Chekhov's *The Three Sisters* and Thornton Wilder's *Our Town* are two plays in which the will is not embodied in a character. Neither play has a protagonist. The will, the driving force, moves outside the characters as the passage of time exerting pressure on the characters. This is not to say that the will is disembodied. In Chekhov's play, we become aware of it first through sound effects, then by the glancing blows time deals to the sisters as they dream of going to Moscow. In Wilder's play, the stage context and the character of the stage manager help us sense the force at work. And whereas some plays lack protagonists, even more lack antagonists. Melodramas almost invariably have them, but more subtle plays may rely on contrary forces within the protagonist, or in adverse circumstance, or in concrete obstacles. Moreover, the audience always exerts a certain force in any play, sometimes strongly enough to be reckoned with. A brilliant example of this occurs in Molière's *Tartuffe,* in which the audience in its superior wisdom invades the stage by proxy in the character of the king's officer to put Orgon's world to rights.

Instead of "conflict," "tension" may be a more apt and all-inclusive term. Tension begins with the polarity between spectacle and spectator and is elaborated in a variety of other forms: contrasts, disparities, incongruities, and ironies, as well as conflicts. Here, drama is clearly distinct from actuality. Life itself may from time to time exhibit all these forms of tension, but drama uses them to catch and hold audience attention. Drama derives its core purpose from its audience—someone has to be watching. Lines of tension, of course, will emerge when there is conflict among characters, but they may also derive from forces exerted out of the characters' past lives, out of another room or another city, out of the sheer passage of time, out of allusions to the world beyond the theatre and many other sources. Tensions arise not only from the movement of the play in time but also from its spatial context, the way stage space is defined. It is the organizing of these lines of tension that renders the play's action coherent, comprehensible, and analyzable. Moreover, every play has a unique way of organizing tensions. No two plays do it exactly the same way. This is also what makes every play different from actuality.

Our task in analysis of a script is to isolate the lines of tension that are sustained, varied, and meaningful for the play's overall effect. Once we find them, we can then quite readily discover why those lines were manipulated that way, which is tantamount to saying that we can discover what the play is about.

Script, Play, and Audience

We can discern three distinct phases to the experience of dramatic art. The first of these is the script, the blueprint for the realization of a play. As noted earlier, this is paradoxically both unrealized and complete. The script is unrealized in the sense that it is simply a plan for a full work of dramatic art and that can happen only once the script moves onto the stage and becomes a play. The script is complete in the sense that it accounts for every factor pertinent and crucial to the play's experience. As a play, the drama consists of the performance of costumed actors moving about within a setting under lights and before a gathered audience. The play, in other words, consists of the stage space and actors' movements, gestures, business, and words spoken in that space. Everything they do is intended to play on the audience's sensibilities and imagination. It is there we find the third and final experience of the play. The audience takes in the play and transforms it with the power of empathy and suspended disbelief into a fuller, richer virtual experience that may then illuminate some facet of their lives.

Chapter Two elaborates on the topic of the audience. For the time being, it is reassuring to note that both the play and the audience are fully implicit in the script. If this were not the case, it would be impossible not only to analyze a script, but also to put on a play using a script as the starting point. Both of these things, however, can be done and are being done all the time. Any time we read a play we are making decisions about its staging as we read, and we are sensing the effects of the imagined world as the audience will encounter it. We examine it with at least some awareness of its design for the stage. The more methodical and thorough we make that examination, the more efficiently and effectively the analysis process will be.

To use an analogy—perhaps slightly far-fetched—analyzing a script might be compared to the efforts that an alien, newly arrived on Earth, might go through on finding a bicycle lying on the ground. The first conclusion would be that this is clearly a device, the product of some designing intelligence. If so, it must be meant to accomplish some function. What function could that be? The alien would go through a series of hypotheses looking for possible explanations that account for the several parts that make up the total bicycle. Setting it upright on its back, the alien would note that turning the crank causes the back wheel to spin, and so it might leap to the conclusion that the bicycle is a wind-making machine. That, however, would not explain the other wheel, which simply sits there. What's more, the bicycle is not very stable sitting on its handle bars and saddle, and the spokes are not shaped appropriately for throwing the air out as wind. Other hypotheses would follow until the alien discovered that turning the bicycle the other side up, sitting on its saddle, and pushing on the pedals will transport a person forward.

Then all the parts are accounted for—the design makes sense. A play script is also the product of a designing intelligence. The job of the analyst is to account for its several parts in terms of the functions they will serve for the play as a whole.

We might profitably refine the three phases of script, play, and audience by seeing the process as a cycle. It begins in the mind of the playwright and comes to rest in the collective mind of the audience. In the clock diagram in Figure 1.3, we can chart the passage of an idea into its existence as a script, from there to its realization on stage, and then into the collective imagination of the audience, finally coming to rest again as the idea. At twelve o'clock on the chart, the playwright has found some facet of human experience intriguing, probably because it already has some strong dramatic expression in his or her mind. Working with that material, wrestling it into various different shapes, the playwright writes until the material finally emerges at two o'clock as a play script. That script is taken up by a group of theatre artists, chief among them the director, and between all the collaborators an approach is taken to the staging of the work. By four o'clock, the designs have been worked out and the actors are rehearsing. The curtain goes up at six o'clock. It is now a play. Between six and eight o'clock, the audience takes the signs and hints offered from the stage (visual and aural elements, physical activity, words spoken) and creates from them the imagined existence of the characters. At that point, the play assumes a full life of its own. At ten o'clock, the audience begins to test the imagined world against life itself, against the audience's sense of reality. Audience members do this partly out of awareness of such aesthetic factors as form, style, and tone. Finally, toward the end of the eleventh hour, the audience arrives at the play's final effect, which actually can happen some time after the curtain has gone down. This again is some facet of human experience that, we may hope, is as intriguing to the audience as it was to the playwright, even if it cannot experience exactly the same perception. This in fact is one of the joys of theatre art: It continu-

FIGURE 1.3   The cycle model of the three phases of the drama.

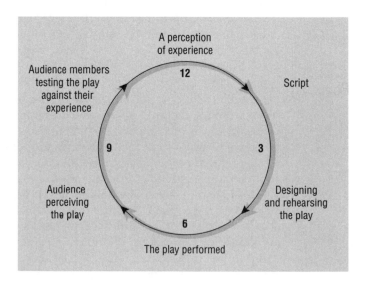

ally renews itself in new stagings with new audiences. If the play script has any dimension to it, any depth, it may reverberate for years and even centuries after it was originally composed, sometimes taking on meanings and values the playwright would not have known were there. In his eloquent essay "Visitations," Jean Giraudoux speaks of a play's journey out into the world:

> From the first performance on, it belongs to the actors. The author wandering in the wings is a kind of ghost whom the stagehands detest if he listens in or is indiscreet. After the hundredth performance, particularly if it is a good play, it belongs to the public. In reality the only thing the playwright can call his own are his bad plays.

There is an issue we need to address: the inherent subjectivity of the dramatic experience. It is not possible for there ever to be a true equation between the idea the playwright had of the play while writing the script and the idea that the audience takes away from the play's performance on stage. Nor is there any absolute correspondence between the meaning or significance one audience member and another finds in the play. One audience member may be intensely moved because of personal experiences like those of one character, while the person in the next seat remains relatively impassive to it, and the one on the other side becomes irritated because it all seems so forced and unnatural, that person never having had an experience of this sort at all. Plays, after all, are not treatises attempting to make a point. To alter a famous saying, plays do not mean, they just are. This should not be an argument for aesthetic solipsism. In other words, this does not mean that every person who witnesses a play has as valid an idea of its structure, form, and meaning as anyone else. Nor does it mean that there is no way to analyze a play script. It does mean that we have to apply a disciplined subjectivity to the examination of a script. Any idea we may have about its effects needs to pass the test of relevance to the total play's inherent structure and sustained patterns. These are discoverable. Like the analogical bicycle, a script is the product of a designing intelligence. At least we have the advantage of knowing that it is intended for production. What else it may be intended for we should be able to discover through a close and rigorous examination of its component parts.

Four Guidelines for Analysis

Following is a set of four fundamental understandings that can guide us in the process of analyzing play scripts. These understandings build on one another as basic assumptions about the nature of drama.

1. *The script must be viewed on its own terms.*
   This assumption grows out of the fact that every script is a contrivance. It is neither actuality nor everyday life. The script is a creation, a recasting of human experience in the distinct medium of the stage. As such, it operates on its own terms. We need to respect those terms if we are to get at the core of the dramatic experience that the script is designed to create. Let the script be what it is. This is

not always easy, but at least we ought to be able to avoid forcing on the script our ideas about what we think it *ought* to be. This is working with "preferred hypotheses," as R. S. Crane would call them. Even if it were statistically true that most towers are phallic symbols and most caves are womb symbols, we are not justified in calling them that unless we find support for it in the text. This is a basic principle of New Criticism, and a valid one. New Criticism argues that everything pertinent to a text is *in* the text. In the case of the drama, however, one factor does in a sense stand outside the text: namely, the audience. On the other hand, the audience is implicitly a part of the script.

2. **a.** *All elements of the script are intentional and of significance in varying degrees.*
   b. *The effort of analysis is to discover the design that informs these elements.*

Naturally, some of the elements of a script may be incidental, but most elements will be crucial to the overall experience of a play, elements that will have to be present if the play is to succeed on its own terms. The fact that different elements are important to varying degrees makes it possible to produce one script in many different ways, all of them equally respectful of the terms on which the play is to operate. This has been aptly demonstrated through the years in productions of the works of William Shakespeare. Max Reinhardt's production of *A Midsummer Night's Dream* did not look a bit like Peter Brook's, and yet both maintained those elements that were crucial to the play. In other words, we need to look for *what matters* in a specific play script. The test for that is what sheds the most light on its experience as a whole. Plays, we should recognize, work by deliberately affecting people. How the play outlined in script form is intended to affect the audience is discoverable by looking for patterns in the manipulation of the medium. This is not to be confused with the "intentional fallacy" that Wimsatt and Beardsley attacked so effectively in their famous essay with that same title. Their argument—the very basis of the New Criticism—was that a literary work contains its own patterns and designs and these are enough to allow analysis. The author's intentions are irrelevant. Thus, we are not interested in what the playwright's personal thoughts may have been during the composing of a script. That is, we are not interested in what the playwright's personal intention may have been. The playwright has created a script, and theoretically it ought to speak for itself. In fact, sometimes a playwright may have lost any firm sense of what he or she thought the play was about. Others refuse any comment on what their plays might mean. As Samuel Beckett so eloquently pointed out, *Waiting for Godot* is about "waiting for Godot." We are interested in the internal design of the script; we do not have to go inside the head of the playwright to find that.

3. **a.** *The playwright writes with the stage in mind.*
   b. *The script contains, implicitly if not explicitly, all clues as to its stage existence.*

These two assumptions recognize that the script is meant as a plan for the realization of the play. The playwright normally calculates effects bearing in mind the open, three-dimensional space of the stage, the physical presence of actors, and the act of presentation they must make to an audience. That being the case, it may not be enough to study just the dialogue. Much happens between the lines. Stage directions may have hidden values affecting rhythms or sudden changes in tone that we need to make ourselves sensitive to. When we watch a play, we are always alive to the look of the play and to its uses of space but these we might miss reading a script. It requires a special effort to keep alert to how the stage medium is to be used for the play that the script is only describing. This is no doubt the reason that many scripts "play well, but read poorly," as many people like to say. Scripts read poorly only because we do not read the script with the stage in mind. Despite the seeming difficulty of this task, it is doable. The clues are all there in the script. They can help us recognize how the immediate stage performance will engender a virtual, fictional experience.

4. **a.** *A play attains its full effect in its encounter with its audience.*
    b. *Its ultimate and most meaningful existence resides in the collective mind of the audience.*
    c. *The total effect of the play is greater than the sum of its parts.*

As mentioned previously, the audience is crucial to the drama. If everything done to create a play is ultimately intended to affect an audience, then the fullest impact and significance are found in the interaction between audience and play. It is first of all the audience's capacity to translate the actual performance into a virtual life for the characters, and then the audience's recognition in that virtual life of values and meanings, that truly complete a play. When the curtain goes down or the stage lights go out and we sense a palpable shock wave roll over the audience, we know that the play has struck a responsive chord. We would know it too if the audience abruptly bounds to its feet with cheers and vigorous applause. Sometimes a play has such an extraordinary economy of effect that we are surprised to look back at how few words or actions contributed to the overwhelming effect. A good example is the storm scene in *King Lear*, a powerful scene observers cannot forget once they have seen the play well produced. Lear and his fool, buffeted about in the winds of the thunderstorm as Lear loses his bearings, his very sanity, and his fool undercuts him with ironic and pithy remarks, together constitute an unforgettable image. Yet the scene is brief. We enlarge it partly by creating in our imaginations a much more desolate and stormy place than the stage can ever be, and partly by empathetically entering into the madness of Lear. We also enlarge it because we recognize in Lear's fall powerful parallels with the experience of rulers and of fathers in general. This scene and our response to it is an example of how the total effect of a play can be greater than the sum of its parts. This may not, of course, be true of very bad plays, which often accumulate so many meaningless details that the sum of the parts far exceeds the total effect.

One note of caution here: None of this should be taken to mean that the process of analyzing scripts is also a process of improving on them. The fact that we seek out the internal design of a play as it relates to its audience does not mean that we can make a coherent play out of a nonsensical pastiche. If we are faced with such a play, the only design we will find in it is one that is so far reaching and out of focus that it carries little significance. This is a matter for the critic to decide. Analysis, although it is crucial to good criticism, is not the same thing as criticism.

All of this means that we need to devote some serious consideration to the involvement of the audience. This is not really a violation of the first assumption, which is that we take the play on its own terms. Writing with the stage in mind means writing with the audience in mind. The audience is very much a part of the terms of the play. New Criticism, with its insistence on examining only the text of a literary work, may let us down on this score, creating a lack that semiotics and readers response theory have attempted to correct. In the theatre, we ignore the audience only at the peril of the play. For that reason, we now turn our attention to the audience.

2 Playwright and Audience

In any play, there are always two more characters than those listed in the cast: the playwright and the audience. Neither of these actually appears on stage and yet they exert a strong influence on the play. In fact, the play is different because of them. Their personalities alter the play, sometimes in fundamental ways. The audience, for its part, may begin as an amorphous, anonymous entity, but gradually its members assume a personality as they become involved in the play. Ideally, the personality of the playwright will merge with that of the audience, at least in the case of a truly engaging play. This occurs because the business of playwriting involves characterizing not only the characters in the play but also the audience attending the play. As we have seen already, drama is not drama without an audience.

Shared Tone

When we attend a play, we are always at least vaguely aware of the contriver and manipulator operating behind the scenes: the playwright. *Vaguely* is actually a key word here. We are vaguely aware of the playwright because we come to share the tone, or the attitude, toward the material that he or she entertained while writing the play. We find that tone comfortable and revealing and so gladly participate in it. Of course, this does not always happen. Many plays remind us painfully of the contriver. Some may even require that the audience assume an attitude that at least some audience members find uncomfortable. To an extent, this is a matter of personal taste. One individual may sit among others who are laughing at a spectacle that strikes that individual as intensely painful or heart wrenching. In such a circumstance, the play is asking the audience member to assume a personality that is alien or even repugnant, and the only recourse is to leave the theatre. Putting aside those instances of personal taste, it ought to be possible to gain insight into how the audience relates to the spectacle. What is the tone we are expected to share in any given play? How is that tone shaped?

The answers are discoverable in the design of the play. Constructing a play means engaging energies, some of which come from the audience. When this is successful, we watch the play through the eyes of the dramatist. In some cases, a scene that seems trivial and inconsequential in the hands of one playwright can become poignant and moving in the hands of another. A comparison of Shakespeare's plays with their sources can be revealing on this score. Every dramatist implicitly chooses an audience. The collection of individuals who flock to a play by Neil Simon is clearly not the same as the group gathered to witness a new piece by Caryl Churchill, and neither of these is the same as the crowd that flocks to the newest installment of *The Lord of the Rings*. Implicitly choosing an audience is tantamount to characterizing the audience. Some of the same individuals may be present in all three audiences, but they change and assume the collective character with the others present by sharing the playwright's tone. Some characters in plays fully engage our empathy and yet, if we were actually to meet them as real people, we would find them annoying, irritating, or even disgusting. This might be said, for example, of Blanche DuBois from Tennessee Williams's *A Streetcar Named Desire*, or Willy Loman from Arthur Miller's *Death of a Salesman*, or Stanley Weber from Harold Pinter's *Birthday Party*, or Uncle Peck (charming though he may be on the surface) from Paula Vogel's *How I Learned to Drive*. For that matter, who would want to meet King Lear face to face? Nevertheless, we relish our encounters with these individuals on stage because we come to share the vision and compassion of the playwright.

Part of the pleasure we derive from attending a play is seeing the world through another person's—the playwright's—eyes. The old adage has it that "there is nothing new under the sun." Probably every kind of dramatic situation has already been attempted by more than one dramatist in the history of the world. Carlo Gozzi declared in the eighteenth century that there are, after all, only thirty-six dramatic situations, and every play is simply some variation on them. This so intrigued Georges Polti in the nineteenth century that he wrote a book titled *The Thirty-Six Dramatic Situations*, in which he cataloged all thirty-six of them and grouped the corresponding plays under each one. Chances are Gozzi was joking, but it is certainly true that the number is limited. What gives a play its freshness is the perspective, the point of view, the tone, that the author brings to it. No one sees the world in exactly the same way. The style that a playwright adopts is determined by how that person sees the world. Clearly, Neil Simon sees it one way, David Mamet another, Peter Barnes still another; Dario Fo, Tennessee Williams, Caryl Churchill, Maria Irene Fornes—all of them have distinctive and recognizable styles. Characterization, the rhythms of the dialogue, the uses of symbols, and the incorporation of the audience are all open to expression, and they become vivid indicators of what we call a playwright's style. In some measure, style is second nature, a product of the playwright's personality, but it is also practiced and polished over the writer's career. It is both instinctual and intensely disciplined. An examination of the evolution of a well-established playwright's style shows both that instinctual quality, which shows up in favored ways of representing human experience, and the discipline, which sharpens and refines the manner of its presentation.

An excellent example comes from British playwright Harold Pinter. In his plays, Pinter tends to create an appearance of ordinary reality; everything seems quite normal. But then he introduces intruding, mysterious, ominous forces that ruffle the superficial realism. We become aware of a menacing undercurrent that eventually bursts through the surface. Plays such as *The Birthday Party, Homecoming, The Caretaker,* and *Old Times* baffle many viewers. By his own account, Pinter has often been asked on lecture tours just what his plays mean. On one such occasion, someone rose in the audience after his lecture and asked the familiar question: "Really, Mr. Pinter, what are your plays about?" Feeling impish and just a little tired of the old question, Pinter replied, "They are about the weasel under the coffee table." As Pinter tells this story, he meant nothing by the remark, although he surely must have known that it was provocative. Later he was surprised when several critical and learned commentaries appeared applying the image of the weasel under the coffee table to the plays of Harold Pinter. His account makes the scholars sound absurd. On the other hand, impish and offhand as the remark had been, it sprang spontaneously to his mind: It was a natural or instinctual expression of his way of seeing things. Moreover, it really does correspond to the well-developed menace that Pinter places beneath the placid surface of his plays.

Drama and the Crowd

Drama depends on a crowd. The crowd may be small and intimate, but it is still a crowd. The very act of gathering and sharing an experience undergirds the dramatic experience. Not so in the case of the short story or the novel. For a reader enjoying a novel, the experience is solitary. He or she reads at whatever pace is comfortable, even jumping forward or backward at will. The entire novel is there between the covers of the book and available at all times, beginning, middle, and end. But a play exists in its own time and we must take it in during that time. The end will come only when it is time for it to come.

This one factor has many implications. It suggests that the drama depends on a sense of spontaneity and immediacy; that it must move forward by engaging our collective imagination, sensibility, and intelligence; that it is an art form that is both aesthetic and social in nature; and that it partakes of a sense of occasion, or festival, a kind of artistic communion. We are concerned here with this last implication.

Anyone who has ever acted on the stage knows the empty feeling that comes at dress rehearsals, at least in the case of a well-prepared play. It all seems such a useless enterprise. Actors speak of this feeling as "hungering for an audience." The play is literally only half there; without its "better half," its audience, it seems dead. The next night, when the audience arrives, the circuit is completed and the play is charged with new energy. It is alive. Thornton Wilder, in "Some Thoughts on Playwriting," has some valuable insights into this condition:

> The theatre partakes of the nature of festival. Life imitated is life raised to a higher power. In the case of comedy, the vitality of these pretended surprises, deceptions, and *contretemps* becomes so lively that before a spectator, solitary or regarding himself as solitary, the structure of so much event would inevitably expose the artificiality of the attempt and ring hollow and unjustified; and in the case of tragedy, the accumulation of woe and apprehension would soon fall short of conviction.

Indeed, there is something fundamentally different about an individual who joins an audience and that same individual alone with a novel. The occasion, the confinement in an auditorium for the duration with fellow audience members, creates a quiet sense of anonymity. One ceases to be an individual in some measure, merging one's identity with those of others. In recompense, the sharing of the experience enhances and enlarges it. A pleasure comes from the combustion of emotional response. And this response comes not only from merging oneself with the crowd, but it also derives from participating in the spectacle itself and especially its performers. We as audience members encounter matters occurring among the characters in the same moment that they encounter them. It is not unusual, as we shall see, for us to respond in a manner contrary to the way the characters respond. We, along with the playwright, may have a different perspective, often a wiser or better informed one, than that allowed the characters. When, for example, we witness Oedipus and the chorus jubilant over the news of the death of his supposed father in Corinth, we know better, and we as an audience experience a very different response.

Drama as Both Aesthetic and Social Event

This brings us to recognize that a play operates on multiple levels, some of them deriving from its artistic and formal construction and some from the social context in which it occurs. Two kinds of reality exist side by side. One is the reality of the theatrical environment: the playhouse auditorium and its gathered audience, the stage and its assembled actors, and the actual activity in which they engage. The other is the reality of the play's imagined world: the characters and their rooms and places and the virtual life they follow. We might think romantically of the second as annihilating the first so that we forget we are in a theatre and think of these characters as people. In truth, these two realities hold each other in suspension. This is, we might remind ourselves, the spirit of willing suspension of disbelief. Robert Benedetti, in his book *The Actor at Work*, argues that we should "abandon the distinction between reality and illusion, and instead speak of various levels of reality that co-exist within the theatre, each of which contacts the audience in its own way and for its own purpose, but interacts with other realities." Nothing, as it turns out, is purely illusion. The fact that a play can set up such a rich reverberation between its several levels of reality gives it the potential for dramatic excitement.

Seen in this way, the audience is anything but a passive, receptive mass of humanity; it is part of the play. Not only do audience members interact with one another and the performers, but they also collaborate in creating the world of the play. Their collective imagination shapes the very places the characters occupy. The audience even completes the characters by responding to the signs the actors provide. Moreover, the audience is constantly testing the world of the play against its sense of the larger reality the play refers to. The play becomes truly engaging when audience members find in it some vibrant correlation to their own experiences. On this score, we can discuss the audience as a "character" in the play. The play is built to arouse, involve, move, and compel its audience, which thereby assumes character.

Following are two contrasting examples of the engagement of the audience's creative energies. The first comes from a highly theatrical play and the other from a realistic play. Dario Fo, one of Italy's most significant playwrights, has written a delicious satire on the exploits of Christopher Columbus, a play titled *Isabella, Three Sailing Ships and a Con Man* (or *Isabella, tre caravelle e un cacciaballe*). The setting is a bare platform placed on the stage in the midst of a Renaissance false-perspective cityscape. The platform is at first the stage for a group of traveling players, but it is subsequently transformed into several different scenes: Ferdinand and Isabella's courtroom, decorated with hanging heraldic banners from staffs; a gallows, replete with hanging nooses; and Columbus's ship, with sails hanging from the staffs. When Columbus puts out to sea, he and his sailors stand on the platform waving to the lords and ladies of the Spanish court, who stand on a rolling platform in front of the "ship." As the ship pulls away from port, stagehands pull the rolling platform offstage by means of a great rope while the lords and ladies wave their handkerchiefs to Columbus. Once at sea, a wild storm erupts. Ellipsoidal spotlights flash, the thunder sheet is shaken, and sailors bounce about on the platform trying to keep their bearings. A group of stagehands run across the stage with an enormous sheet, which they unfold and shake to create great billowing waves of the angry sea. Some sailors fall overboard and drown, and we then see them crawling offstage under the sheet's waves. Never for a moment does the audience forget the "social reality" of the platform, the rope, the thunder sheet, the flashing lights, or the shaken sheet; but the audience also creates with those items another reality, in its way just as real, of a dockside farewell and a great storm at sea. A side effect of this creative participation is that we begin to view the story of Christopher Columbus with a stronger awareness of the world around us and become more sensitive to the capitalistic and imperialistic forces that have co-opted this hero of the New World.

We might assume that the audience watching a realistic play would make only minimal creative contribution to it. After all, if the theatre artists have taken pains to make the world of the play look and sound as much like life itself as possible, what is left for the audience to contribute? Actually, it may contribute a great deal. The opening scene of Anton Chekhov's *The Three Sisters* provides a good example. The setting is a drawing room downstage and an alcove dining area upstage. As the play opens, the three sisters, Olga, Masha, and Irina, are in the downstage area. Moments later, three military men, Tusenbach, Soliony, and Chebutykin, enter the alcove area and sit at the table where they engage in their own conversation, oblivious of the women. We hear only bits and pieces of their talk. Meanwhile, we hear two of the sisters talk about Moscow:

OLGA: Eleven years have gone by, but I remember everything as if we'd only left there yesterday. Oh, my goodness! I woke this morning, the sun was blazing. I could feel that spring was here. And I did so long to be home again.

CHEBUTYKIN: You've gone out of your mind.

TUSENBACH: It's all nonsense, of course.

(Masha, engrossed in her book, quietly humming.)

OLGA: Masha. Don't hum. How can you! *(Pause.)* School all day, private lessons all evening, so I have headaches all the time. I'm beginning to feel quite old. Shall I tell you something? Every single day of the four years at the high school, minute by minute, I have felt my strength and my youth draining away. And only one dream kept growing stronger and stronger.

IRINA: To go to Moscow! To sell the house, make an end of everything here, and . . . Moscow.

(Chebutykin and Tusenbach laugh.)

IRINA: Brother will be a professor most likely, so he won't be staying here. The one thing in the way is poor Masha.

OLGA: Masha will spend the whole summer in Moscow every year.

(Masha whistles.)

IRINA: It will all be arranged, if God wills.

As it happens, God does not will. Despite the almost desperate longing Olga and Irina have to go to Moscow, they remain so distracted by the little events of their life in a small town that neither they nor anyone else does what would need to be done to move back to the city of their dreams. Somehow we know they will never actually go there. Part of the reason we know comes from the little undercuts printed in italic. The remarks and laughter of the men and the humming and whistling of Masha have nothing to do with Irina and Olga's conversation. Nevertheless, these elements punctuate the sisters' exchange in such a way as to suggest that for all their talk of going to Moscow, they never will. Chekhov does not say so. Even the three men do not say so. Nor does Masha. We say so. The rest of the play will bear us out, and we can congratulate ourselves on being so perceptive. This is a play about the passage of time, which can make decisions for anyone who is not attentive. We sense this from the beginning, and in doing so we are collaborating as creatively with Chekhov as we do with Fo in the previous example.

The point here is that the audience contributes to a play. Any analysis of a play script that fails to take into account the nature of the audience's role in the play is doomed to fall short. A play is in fact partially created by the audience. Interacting with the play on the social level actually serves to create the aesthetic level. The play's virtual life and its effects are products of the interaction between spectacle and spectator, and thus the play is not fully realized until it encounters its audience. This is not to say that we must wait to observe an audience before declaring its involvement. Audience involvement is built into the play's experience and is evident within the script itself.

Drama's Dependence on Polarity

An intriguing interplay of levels of experience characterizes the audience's engagement with a play. The audience's reality is set against the reality of the play; one character's reality may play against another's; the world onstage may be in sharp contrast to the fictional world beyond our view; the present time may be in sharp contrast to the past; the future the characters expect may diverge powerfully from what we know to be their future; one character may be at odds with another, and so forth. Contrasts, opposites, disparities, incongruities, ironies, conflicts—these are the stuff of drama, the source of its fascination. At the base of all these is **polarity:** tension drawn between two poles. Polarity is the basic dramatic device; plays are built on it. Polarity creates the energy system that binds together and enlivens a play. It is the material the playwright uses in constructing drama. As we have seen before, the spirit of encounter informs all drama. It begins when spectator meets spectacle. That creates the first tension. That polarity is enlarged, varied, and elaborated from that time forward.

In the first chapter, five characteristics of the dramatic mode were listed. The first two are of special note here: (1) the first and most basic ingredient in the dramatic mode is the **encounter,** and (2) **polarity and tension** provide the fundamental dramatic device. Polarity and tension are a natural outgrowth of the motif of encounter. A play entails the encounter between two worlds: the world of the play itself and the world of the audience. When an audience gathers and individuals take their seats before a closed curtain, they bring with them all the mundane concerns that color the day that has just passed. Some have had problems at the office or at work, some with their automobiles, others with a friend or a lover, still others with their bankbooks. Some arrive as individuals, some as couples, and some in parties of friends. Yet they all bring a generally shared understanding of the world they live in, the world we all live in. More than that, by virtue of their shared humanity they bring with them the concerns that attach to the very act of living: fear, uncertainty, love, joy, hope, and despair. With the dimming of the light, a hush falls on the audience. Conversations cease; all attention is riveted on the stage as the curtain rises. This is one of those exciting moments everyone relishes. In a bad play, of course, the opening is the most exciting moment, and perhaps the only exciting moment. A good play, however, builds on that initial tension.

What makes the initial moment so exciting is the wonderful promise: Anything is possible. A wholly new world is about to unfold. Those living, breathing actors up on that stage will begin to induce in us a vision of another life. Herein lies the key to how plays multiply tensions. The first source is simply the act of presentation: performers in some setting presenting themselves to us. The second source is the provocative and intriguing disparity between the actual performance of actors on stage and the virtual activity of characters in their own world. They can never be exactly the same. Moreover, neither of the two ever ceases to exist in our minds. They maintain themselves in a state of suspension throughout the play. This, of course, is willing suspension of disbelief, the result of the contrary pull of empathy against aesthetic distance. In the next instance, we witness the overt behavior of the characters and recognize in it something of their inner lives; potentially there may be tension here as well, a tension between what a character may do and what the character desires. When we combine our imagination, which enables us to produce a virtual existence for the characters, with our sensitivity to the characters' motivations and drives, we become fully engaged with the play. The play comes to life, we might say. From that time on, we look for further elaborations of tensions as characters deal with their pasts, with the obstacles in the lives they lead, with one another, and even in some ways with us.

The Opacity–Transparency Principle

The three stages of artistic creation outlined by Suzanne Langer in *Feeling and Form* are enlightening about this connection between play and audience. She speaks of these as steps in the process of creating a work of art, but they are equally valid as phases in the audience's perception of a work of art, especially of a play. The first stage is the deliberate separation of the artwork from actuality. By various formal means, the audience is alerted not to mistake the realm of the artwork with that of the real world. The frame around a painting asks us not to confuse the painting with the wall. The same applies to the pedestal for a sculpture, the arrangement of words on a page for a poem, the coda in music, and the proscenium arch for plays. All art starts there: It asks us to regard something in a new way simply by divorcing it from life. On our part, we acknowledge the right of the artwork to exist independently from ordinary, everyday experience. We are therefore willing to contemplate it. At this point the artwork remains **opaque,** consisting of surface display. We recognize it as something to be contemplated and know that it is the product of creative endeavor. Should an artist take a greasy differential from a junkyard, put it on a pedestal, and label it "The Modern World," only the first stage of artistic creation has been completed, not the other two. Viewing the "sculpture," we remain unmoved and disinterested. The piece is opaque and relatively dead.

The second stage involves the manipulation of the material of the artwork to produce an **illusion.** Elements are arranged to allow us to see through the piece of art into a realm beyond it—in the case of drama, into the virtual world of the characters of the play. The artwork has become at least partially transparent. While this happens, we remain cognizant that the artwork still exists on a somewhat different plane. We can sense not only the imagined domain, but even some feeling of vicarious experience, sharing the characters' lives and emotions. Again, however, the artwork often stops at this point. The action painter, for example, draws attention to the manipulation of the materials of the medium of painting, and we in turn share some of the energy that went into it. Still, the transparency of the artwork is by no means complete. In the case of the theatre, some instances of performance art call such attention to the manipulation of the materials that the artwork remains relatively opaque. Certainly, for an audience unaware of the conventions involved, a performance of Noh drama out of traditional Japanese theatre may be fascinating for the masks, colors, music, a stylized movement, but such an audience can enjoy only these formal elements, leaving the play relatively opaque even if they can follow the story line.

Langer's third stage is the **emergence of transparency.** Once we have exercised our imaginations to create the illusion of the fictional world of the play, through the medium and the illusion we gain an insight into reality itself. The separation of the artwork from actuality and the manipulation of the medium are formal and technical matters done ultimately to create an effect on the audience.

When successful, that effect causes us to see our lives in a slightly new light. Opacity fades; the work of art becomes a sort of lens for viewing the world as we might never have seen it before. Everything done in the name of art is meant to affect us, and the most meaningful effects are those that move us to some new recognition. We may remain fully aware that it is a contrived work, the product of calculated manipulations, but we also arrive at a vivid sense of the human experience. Knowing the formal elements of the medium used need not preclude our ability to recognize its reflection of reality; in fact, it may even enhance our enjoyment.

When we come to know an excellent play well, it is always a surprise to discover how little in the script could inspire so much. Seemingly few words and little activity can sometimes summon up a rich experience. The gap between what is literally there and the full experience is filled with contributions we ourselves have made in our imaginations and sensitivities. The storm scene in *King Lear* mentioned earlier is a case in point. It is vivid, exciting, and even disturbing, yet it is also brief. Moreover, what we actually see on stage consists merely of two men shouting over thunder sound effects. We imagine the full heath and all the wind and rain. We also provide an awareness of the mental anguish that feeds into the scene. We as audience complete it. The three stages of artistic creation are complete at that moment.

Histrionic Sensibility

Human beings possess two faculties that are crucial to the experience of drama. Indeed, without them drama could not exist. The first is imagination. Imagination frees us to transcend what we see and hear on the stage to give it a palpable virtual existence. We can take what an actor does and translate it into what the character does. The suggestions evident in the scenery prompt a full vision of the world of the play. This is what Brecht has called the "naïveté" of the theatre experience: It is the childlike capacity we all have in some measure to imagine what is not there. Should anyone lose that capacity, he or she could no longer experience theatre.

The second is **histrionic sensibility.** This term, coined by Francis Fergusson and described in his book *The Idea of Theatre*, refers to that innate human faculty to grasp the meaning of the actions of others. *Histrionic* comes from the Etruscan word for performance and *sensibility* of course means "awareness"; so literally the phrase means "awareness of performance." Histrionic sensibility is our ability to recognize the feelings and intentions of other people by such clues as vocal intonation, eye activity, facial expression, and body language, especially taken in context. Again, without this faculty, drama would not be possible.

Drama, in all its forms, is objective: It plays directly on our senses of sight and sound. The audience can glimpse the inner lives of the characters only by what they see them do and say (or, more precisely, what they see the actors do and say). The novelist can describe the inner workings of a character's mind directly, but the playwright has no such luxury. On the stage, the character becomes clear only through the actions and reactions and interactions we can actually witness. To be sure, a playwright may resort to the device of the soliloquy, but that is a conventional way of objectifying the mind by playing it as at war with itself, mulling and wrestling with the issues at stake. Soliloquy is a convention. It occurs only when a character such as Hamlet experiences such inner turmoil that he must wrestle with his mind. Certainly it cannot be sustained throughout the play. We learn more about Hamlet's true state of mind by seeing him in action than we do by his four soliloquies. An audience can derive as much pleasure from exercising its histrionic sensibility as it does from exercising its imagination. "Reading" the actions of the character— recognizing in the context of the action and in the way the character responds— gives the audience a share in the creative act of theatre.

Suppose you are in the grandstand when a runner slides into third base. You see the umpire's thumb fly up, the runner jump to his feet and stand nose-to-nose with the umpire, his jaw working. You cannot hear a word, and yet you know very well what is happening: Your histrionic sensibility tells you. In private conversation with a friend, you understand each other far more by vocal intonation, eye activity, facial expression, and body language than by the actual words spoken. In the act of living, our histrionic sensibility is constantly engaged. Sometimes our survival depends on it. Drama depends on it too, for it is a powerful link between the play and its audience.

Histrionic sensibility works through two sources: the context and the tone of the action. In the example of the baseball runner, you recognize the meaning of the action partly by the events leading up to it (the intense dash from second to third, the ball fired to the third baseman, the slide to the base) and the rules of the game that apply—all of which constitute context—and partly by the tone of the action (the abrupt way the runner jumps to his feet, the intensity with which he holds his body, the red face and the working jaw). Both context and tone are required for understanding. If the audience is unclear about the context, the tone alone will not convey meaning, and vice versa. Psychologists have shown that a close-up photograph of a face expressing intense emotion cannot be identified as any specific emotion because without the context, one emotion can easily be mistaken for another—ecstasy for pain, for example.

Three examples from stage plays illustrate this. In the very last scene of Shakespeare's *King Lear,* Lear enters carrying the body of Cordelia. From the context, we know that Cordelia is dead, that she was Lear's daughter, and that she had proven her devotion to him despite his rejection of her. We also know the pain his other two daughters have caused him and something of his deep regret over his treatment of Cordelia. In Lear's action, we can sense him grasping at every last shred of hope that she may yet be alive. He tells us so as well, but that is not enough. Shakespeare adds these "histrionic" details:

> LEAR: Howl, howl, howl, howl! O, you are men of stones!
> Had I your tongues and eyes, I'd use them so
> That heaven's vault should crack. She's gone forever!
> I know when one is dead, and when one lives;
> She's dead as earth. Lend me a looking glass;
> If that her breath will mist or stain the stone,
> Why, then she lives.

KENT: Is this the promised end?

EDGAR: Or image of that horror?

ALBANY: Call and cease.

LEAR: This feather stirs; she lives! If it be so,
It is a chance which does redeem all sorrows
That ever I have felt.

KENT: *(Kneeling.)* O my good master!

LEAR: Prithee, away.

EDGAR: 'Tis noble Kent, your friend.

LEAR: A plague upon you, murderers, traitors all!
Cordelia, Cordelia! Stay a little. Ha!
What is't thou say'st? Her voice was ever soft,
Gentle, and low, an excellent thing in woman.

As the scene progresses, Lear becomes distracted with other news, but he returns to Cordelia, seemingly convinced that she may yet be alive:

LEAR: Why should a dog, a horse, a rat, have life,
And thou no breath at all? Thou'lt come no more,
Never, never, never, never, never!
Pray you, undo this button. Thank you, sir.
Do you see this? Look on her, look, her lips,
Look there, look there! *(Dies.)*

These passages contain only two stage directions: "Kneeling" and "Dies." Yet there is a wealth of action in all that is said. We can picture Lear's entrance carrying Cordelia and see in his face the rage he feels at everyone he sees, everyone left living, for each is guilty of outliving her. He moves from rage with "Howl, howl, howl, howl!" to grief with "She's dead as earth," when he must put her on the ground, and then on to hope as he asks for a looking glass. He receives a feather instead. Then Lear must kneel beside Cordelia as he thinks he sees the feather stir and hears her speak. Finally, in his grief he loses all control and must ask someone else to undo his button, which someone does: "Thank you, sir." All these are rich histrionic clues for our sensibility to seize on.

The plays of Anton Chekhov rely heavily on the audience's capacity to read the actions of the characters. Chekhov provides the means to engage histrionic sensibility by carefully shaping the context and then creating an activity that vividly reveals the inner life of the character, often with a degree of comic, yet pathetic, irony. His characters frequently say one thing while performing an activity that contradicts and undermines the statement. If there is a quintessential Chekhovian gesture, it would be the image of a person lying languidly upon a couch declaring that we must all work. Here is an example, again out of *The Three Sisters*. The context of this scene consists of the love affair between Masha and Colonel Vershinin, who is now being transferred to another town, much to the relief of Masha's husband, Kulyghin. The lovers have just said farewell, and Vershinin has gone, as Kulyghin knows full well. Olga, Masha's sister, tries to comfort her when Kulyghin enters:

KULYGHIN: *(Embarrassed.)* It's nothing . . . let her cry . . . let her. You are my own dear Masha, my good, good child . . . you are my wife, and I'm content in spite of all . . . I've no complaints. I am not reproaching you in the least bit. . . . And Olga here knows that's true. We'll start our old life all over again. I won't say a single word to you—not the least hint.

MASHA: *(Trying to control sobs.)* The green oak, the golden chain . . . I'm going out of my mind. . . . The green oak.

OLGA: Control yourself. Pull yourself together. Bring her some water.

MASHA: I'm not crying anymore.

KULYGHIN: She's not crying anymore . . . She's a good, good girl . . .

(Offstage in the distance a pistol shot is heard.)

MASHA: The green oak . . . A green tomcat . . . Green oak . . . I'm all confused. *(Drinks water.)* Empty life . . . I don't need anything now . . . I shall be myself again in a moment . . . It's all the same . . . What is the meaning of curved shore? Why do these words keep haunting me? My mind is in a whirl.

(Irina comes in.)

OLGA: Control yourself, Masha, like a good girl . . . Let's go inside.

MASHA: *(Angrily.)* I won't go in there. *(She begins to cry but immediately checks herself.)* I don't want to go into the house. I won't go into the house.

IRINA: Let's sit together and just say nothing. I'm going away tomorrow.

(Pause.)

KULYGHIN: Yesterday I confiscated this beard and mustache from a boy in grade four. *(Produces them and puts them on.)* Rather like the German teacher, eh? *(He laughs.)* Isn't it so? Aren't boys absolutely killing?

MASHA: You really are like that German of yours.

OLGA: *(Laughs.)* You know, he is!

(Masha weeps.)

IRINA: That'll do, Masha.

KULYGHIN: I really do look like him.

In this sequence, knowing as we do the context for the action, we can sense not only the agony that Masha feels in losing her lover and having to return to her husband, but also the anguish of her husband, Kulyghin. His ridiculous, awkward attempt to win back his wife by playing the buffoon, waving the fake beard in her face, covers his inner anxiety, and yet we can recognize it very well just watching him. It is as though he were saying, "I know I am not much compared to the colonel, but at least I'm amusing." And of course Masha bursts into tears again. Our histrionic sensibility permits us to sense the powerful undercurrent to the scene.

Comic effect too can derive from appeals to histrionic sensibility. In Molière's *Tartuffe*, perhaps the most famous moment is the first entrance of the title character. We have heard Tartuffe spoken of for more than two acts. Some characters have described him as pious, devout, upright, and an example of moral conduct for the entire household to emulate. Others have characterized him as a hypocritical, lecherous scoundrel. As evidence piles up, we tend to agree with the latter group. When he finally enters, we know we are right. As he comes through the door, he sees the maidservant, Dorine, and turns back to call to his servant Laurent, putting on this performance just for her:

TARTUFFE: *(Seeing Dorine.)* Laurent, put away my hairshirt and my scourge and continue to pray Heaven to send you grace. If anyone asks for me, I'll be with the prisoners distributing alms.

DORINE: *(Aside.)* The impudent hypocrite!

TARTUFFE: What do you want?

DORINE: I'm to tell you . . .

TARTUFFE: For Heaven's sake! Before you speak, I pray you take this handkerchief. *(He takes a handkerchief from his pocket.)*

DORINE: Whatever do you mean?

TARTUFFE: Cover your bosom. I can't bear to see it. Such pernicious sights give rise to sinful thoughts.

DORINE: You're mighty susceptible to temptation then! The flesh must make a great impression on you! I really don't know why you should get so excited. I can't say that I'm so easily roused. I could see you naked from head to foot and your whole carcass wouldn't tempt me in the least.

Any doubts we may have had that Tartuffe is a lecherous hypocrite are dispelled within moments of his arrival on stage. The two actions of calling offstage to Laurent and extending the handkerchief to Dorine clinch his true nature. He makes a show of his piety and plainly exhibits his lechery. Again, we recognize all this with the exercise of our histrionic sensibility, especially in the matter of the handkerchief.

Notice too that an aid to engaging the audience's histrionic sensibility is the use of objects or things that force a character to deal with them. The button that needs undoing and the feather in *King Lear*, the false beard and moustache in *The Three Sisters*, and the handkerchief in *Tartuffe* all serve as objective factors that help expose the inner lives of the characters. When characters have to deal with such things, they open themselves to our scrutiny.

Internal Probability

Thus far we have explored two powerful human faculties that enable audience members to engage with a play as they watch it: imagination and histrionic sensibility. Both of them allow the audience to join in the creation of the world of the play. Its members in a very real sense are creative collaborators with the playwright. One other factor serves to engage the audience—namely, **internal probability.** As we have seen, a play separates itself from real life in order to reflect on life. The world of the play is its own distinct realm. As such, it can operate according to its own laws. What is probable or believable in a play is not necessarily probable in the real world. This does not mean that the play avoids dealing with reality (although some do), only that it is free to do so on its own terms. In fact, this freedom makes it possible for the play to reflect much more vividly on the lives we lead. In other words, a play operates according to its own laws, and this we call "internal probability." Understanding a play requires us to accept these laws.

This principle is sometimes called "Aristotelian probability" for the very good reason that Aristotle described it so thoroughly in his *Poetics.* His point is that a play cannot engage an audience unless its action appears plausible, and that in turn depends on what may be probable given the internal laws of the play's world. In fact, it makes no difference if some event is possible in the real world; if it is to occur in a play, it still must be rendered as probable. Aristotle makes this remark about real and fictional probability: In a play, it is far better to have "a probable impossibility than an improbable possibility." Perhaps one of the most remarkable examples of this principle is Eugène Ionesco's play *Rhinoceros,* in which all the citizens of a provincial French town turn into rhinoceroses—all, that is, except the central character, who is left at the end hoping against hope that he can transform too. All of this, of course, is patently impossible in the real world, but we can believe it in the world Ionesco creates. Strangely enough, twisting ordinary probability in this way enables the playwright to reflect on reality in a vivid and compelling way. Masses of people do not transform themselves into rhinoceroses, but the spectacle of their doing so brings to mind experiences we have all had of people around us becoming myopic, beady-eyed, thick-skinned, compassionless monsters driven by the herd instinct. If you have not witnessed it on the sweeping social level of, say, Nazism, you may have seen in it high school cliques.

This means that we must be alert to the clues that appear early in a play as to the nature of its world. Most plays lay this out early. The title, the cast of characters, the description of the set, and the opening action are rich in indications of the world we are experiencing. Ionesco's *The Bald Soprano* is a good case in point: The title suggests something peculiar about this play, which opens with the clock chiming seventeen times. Perhaps the most blatant example is Tom Stoppard's *Rosencrantz and Guildenstern Are Dead.* First of all, the title strikes us as a little strange: We are about to witness a play about two fellows named Rosencrantz and Guildenstern and they are announced at once as being dead. The cast of characters sets these two over against the members of the court of Denmark and the players that come to perform at court, and we sense a certain likelihood that their encounters with these two groups may spell their doom. Finally, the play opens with Rosencrantz and Guildenstern on the forestage tossing coins that keep coming up heads, one after another. This oddity leads Guildenstern into declaring that they must be operating under un-, sub-, or supernatural forces. Only that could explain this phenomenal improbability. Of course, it might also be explained by virtue of their being inside a play.

The Play as a Game

Play is a fundamental human instinct. It is probably no accident that our word for drama is *play*. Johann Huizinga has suggested that the distinguishing factor of our humanity may be our instinct for play, and he calls both his book and the human animal *Homo ludens,* or "playing man," rather than the more familiar *homo sapiens,* or "knowing man." One way in which we humans know is by play. We see this happening whenever a child indulges in play, especially if it involves assuming a role. Role-playing is a way for the child to test reality. This instinct for play has given us games, rituals, ceremonies, and, of course, plays. None of these is necessarily frivolous, but they are infused with a certain spirit of delight as well as discovery.

Comparing drama to games can reveal something of the nature of drama. Like games, plays occupy their own domains or playing fields, operate under their own rules, and assign roles to their participants, who then engage in creating and elaborating tensions. A game first sets itself apart in its own space, "in bounds" as against "out of bounds." It also establishes a fixed time interval for its playing. A game cannot be played except by its own internal rules. The players must abide by those rules and assume field positions and duties accordingly. Their efforts are set against those of their opponents and against the conditions of the field—distances to traverse, nets, or barriers. There is even a degree of pretense involved inasmuch as it must matter that someone wins. Up to this point, plays are very like games. They set themselves apart in their own space and time; they operate under the principle of internal probability, their rules of the game; and they develop and elaborate tensions that arise from antagonists (opponents) or circumstances (conditions of the field.) Plays consist of a driving force that strives toward a goal against all odds. As in a game, that struggle is a source of a certain pleasure.

Differences between games and plays are also revealing and ultimately more important. First of all, plays set themselves apart from mundane actuality not just for the sake of playing the game. They do so in order to reflect on reality. Note the many references Shakespeare makes to this condition: "All the world's a stage," and we are players "who strut our hour upon the stage and then are heard no more"; "Suppose within this wooden O are two mighty monarchies"; and "To hold as 'twere the mirror up to reality." Second, plays depend on pretense. They create illusions. In plays, virtual activity always accompanies actual activity, whereas games consist of purely actual activity. Once there is virtual activity, we can begin to empathize or identify with characters through our faculty of histrionic sensibility. True, we may feel empathy for a player hurt on the field, but the point of a game has nothing to do with our involvement as spectator. As we have seen before, games can be played perfectly well with or without spectators. This leads to the third fundamental difference: Plays depend on the act of presentation. That means they require an audience. Plays simply are not complete until experienced by an audience.

Progression of Audience Involvement

The audience's involvement in a play moves through several phases, expanding as it goes. The following is an account of the progression an audience experiences watching a play:

1. First, audience members gather in the house (auditorium), chatting among themselves, perhaps preoccupied with the day's concerns. They approach the play in a state of open anticipation. They know, or hope, that the spectacle they are about to see will carry them into another realm, into other levels of reality, although they know full well they remain in a theatre. In this other realm, new lives will be glimpsed, as well as new ways of seeing life.

2. As the play begins, the individual audience member assumes a certain anonymity, merging personal identity with the crowd. The gathered audience seeks a kind of communion in the action portrayed on stage, action that seems to raise life to a higher power. Drama depends on group combustion.

3. Now the audience becomes alert to every suggestion and hint from the stage as to the fictional world it is encountering. It then translates the actors' actual activity within some sort of stage setting into virtual activity belonging to the world of the play.

4. The audience begins to take pleasure in "reading" the actions of the characters, finding emotional meaning in them through histrionic sensibility. Observers create the inner life of the play and engage their empathy with it.

5. They relish the immediacy of the moment, the "illusion of the first time," which gives them the sense of spontaneous present time played out before their eyes. It appears to be happening now.

6. They allow themselves to be carried into the play by the interplay of tensions. These may take the form of irony, contrast, disparity, incongruity, or conflict. Audience members bind themselves to the spectacle in the spirit of anticipation, watching a driving force striving against circumstance or contrary wills.

7. As the play begins to assume a recognizable shape, aesthetic distance permits audience members to reflect on their own lives in relation to the play. Once the play rounds out and concludes, its final effect is savored and evaluated. If the tone has been right, the audience takes a certain pleasure in sharing the vision of the playwright. In any event, it is ultimately in the collective imagination, empathy, and vision of the audience that a play truly resides.

At the same time, an audience is never absolutely united with the playwright's tone from beginning to end. Everyone brings his or her own experience and sensibility to the theatre. As a result, one person may respond much more powerfully to a moment in the play than the person in the next seat. Women in the audience will probably react somewhat differently than men to the scene in August Wilson's *Fences* in which Troy Maxson asks his wife to care for the baby he fathered with his now dead mistress. So might black audience members in contrast to white. Nevertheless, this scene generates a basic effect of a pathetic plea for a "motherless child" on the part of this "womanless man." In the case of many postmodern plays, there is frequently a deliberate disparity of responses built into the play. In the case of Heiner Müller's *Hamletmachine,* for example, so many allusions pile up in the course of the play—allusions to things out of Shakespeare's play, out of the destruction and horror of the Second World War, out of the ecological mess of the Earth, out of illness and cancerous diseases—that no one person in the audience can respond exactly like any other person, for no one can recognize all of the allusions, and those that one person does recognize may elicit a reaction different from that of the next person. Still, in this accumulation a pattern emerges that we all share, a pattern reflecting the miserable state of the world.

This progression can be graphically represented in a sort of zigzag pattern, as shown in Figure 2.1. In this representation, the audience on the left-hand side of the diagram encounters the play on the right-hand side. The audience's senses of sight and sound encounter the actual activity of the actors on stage. Everything about that activity and the appearance of the stage can then engage the audience's imagination. The collaboration between the performance and the audience's collective

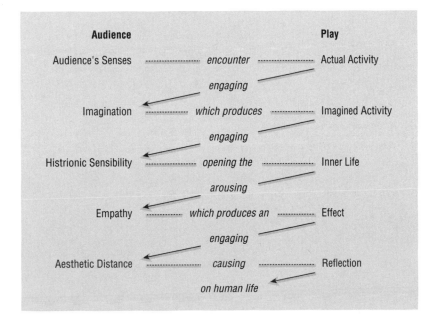

FIGURE 2.1   The zigzag progression of an audience's encounter with a play.

imagination produces the virtual world of the play. Where we have actors on stage, we also now have characters in their own world. These characters play on histrionic sensibility, which opens up their inner lives, and that in turn arouses audience empathy. Empathy produces an effect on us: It moves us to awe, wonder, worry, tears, amusement, or outright laughter. Finally, reminding themselves that this is an art form, audience members admire its work in the spirit of aesthetic distance. That then permits them to test the play's experience against their life experience. They end up reflecting on reality. When all is said and done, plays are *about* the human condition. They are powerful to the degree that they reflect that condition.

CHAPTER 3

The Contextual Dimension of Drama: Spatial and Temporal Isolation

A peculiarity of the drama is its reliance in equal measure on both space and time to create its effects. Most art forms rely much more heavily on one or the other. Painting and sculpture, for example, are essentially spatial arts. The manner in which the artist manipulates space conveys most of the effect. One may speak of the "rhythm" of the composition of a painting, referring to the pattern of movement the eye takes as it surveys the arrangement of the painting's shapes, but the fact remains that it is an arrangement in space. Meanwhile, music is a temporal art, creating effects through changes in tone, rhythm, and tempo. It does enhance one's enjoyment to be in the presence of the musicians in the act of performing, but this is not crucial. In contrast, drama needs both the three-dimensional space of the stage and the duration of activity on that stage to create effect. Movement in space is the very substance of the drama.

This poses a certain problem for script analysis. Reading a script, we are naturally aware of the passage of time—of the creation, sustaining, and variation of tensions. We can readily sense a developing crisis, absorb its impact as it arrives, and feel the tension snap and the resolution ensuing afterward. But connecting with the spatial element of the drama from a script is a much different matter. The script is not the stage. It does not even look like a stage. The medium the playwright had in mind is simply not there on the page. Watching a play, however, we are fully cognizant of its spatial context. The physical relationships between actors at any given moment, the setting in which they move, the implications of space beyond the visible world, and the costumes and properties in use are all there before our eyes. They all contribute to our sense of the virtual world of the characters and ultimately the effect they produce. For this reason, we have to summon up a vision of the stage when studying the script. We must read, in Kenneth Thorpe Rowe's words, with "a theatre in our head."

This double dimension of the drama poses another problem, one that is rather like the problem physicists have describing an atom, which they may treat as particles or as waves, but not at the same time. For the stage, we can certainly gain a sense of the spatial context in which the action of the play will transpire, but we must hold it in mind all the time, for at any one moment in time an effect may derive from it.

For the time being, this chapter explores the spatial and contextual dimension of the stage. We might remind ourselves that a play is by definition "isolated in time and space," in Bernard Beckerman's language. This means that the play's action develops in some sort of restricted space in a time cut off from the characters' past and their future. Something has always happened before. That is true even of *Waiting for Godot:* Vladimir and Estragon were here on this road waiting for Godot yesterday and they'll be back again tomorrow. Marsha Norman's *'night, Mother* plays off the long history of Jessie's life, all the frustrations and disappointments that have led her to the extreme of her announced suicide. "Now" can always be set over against "then." By the same token, the action transpiring on stage, "here," may well be set over against an implicit "there," the world beyond the stage. Dramatic context, then, consists of the isolation of the play's action in both time and space. Unless we take this into account, we may lose many important values inherent in the script. It may be helpful to start with spatial isolation because reading a script requires us first to set in mind the place in which the action will occur. Very soon after, we will become aware of what has happened that bears on the present circumstance. Once we have set the context, then we can follow the developing action, which is the subject of the next chapter: drama's existence in time.

The Stage as Confined Space

The first thing we might observe about the stage is its confinement. This is particularly striking in the case of the proscenium stage. The proscenium arch encases a space set apart from the auditorium to the front and from the wings to each side. The space to be occupied by the performers is very much a confined space. Realists such as Henrik Ibsen made heavy use of that sense of confinement in plays such as *A Doll's House* or *Ghosts,* both of which take place in rooms whose walls cut off the space from all surrounding areas and so give us a strong sense of a life being lived in close quarters. Playwrights such as Harold Pinter and Samuel Beckett use the confinement of space to enhance certain effects. Both of them tend to write for a proscenium stage but for different reasons: Pinter because it suits his interest in developing mysterious and ominous forces emanating out of an off-stage space, a world beyond, and Beckett because his plays represent the parameters of life itself, so that an exit would read as departure from this life, which no one quite wants to do.

The stage can assume many other configurations. Shakespeare and his fellow Elizabethans, as well as many contemporary playwrights, make use of a thrust stage, a platform area that extends out into the auditorium. Such a space may not seem at first glance nearly as confined as the proscenium stage. Indeed, it is not. Nevertheless, it remains a restricted area. Although it is possible for the action on the thrust stage to represent a multitude of different times and places, in any one instance it remains a confined space. In the first two acts of Shakespeare's *Henry V,* we move from one chamber to another in the royal palace in London, to the streets of London, to a council chamber in Southampton, to a London tavern, and to the royal palace and battlefield in France. Each of these scenes gives us the sense of a particular figurative space that is closely confined.

Even more open to all appearances is the arena stage, with audience surrounding it on all sides. In this case, too, the world of the play is restricted to the space set in the midst of the audience, characters (actors) coming from behind the audience to enter into the play's own space. The most open kind of configuration possible is the black box, or environmental space, wherein action may take place now here and now there in the very midst of the audience. Yet even in environmental space, the sense of confinement is maintained. The moment a spectacle attracts the interest of the audience, it isolates itself in its own space. An example of this is *Passion Play,* an adaptation of the medieval mystery plays of England created by Bill Bryden for the National Theatre of Britain. The audience is ambulatory, moving from spectacle to spectacle wherever it may occur. But in every instance, that spectacle is isolated and set apart from the audience. At one point, audience members may be witness to the creation and the emergence of Adam and Eve, at another they may participate in the building of Noah's ark, and still others may be a part of the crowd calling for Barabbas and so condemning Christ. Wherever the spectacle occurs, it sets itself apart from the crowd, calls attention to itself, and works off the sense of isolation or confinement. Thus, even in environmental theatre, where the action transpires in the midst of the audience, the spectacle may be now here, now there, but always isolated the moment it happens.

These various configurations—proscenium, thrust, arena, and black box—are graphically represented in Figure 3.1. Scripts may find their way into production in any one of these configurations. Shakespeare wrote his scripts for the thrust stage of the Elizabethan playhouse, but they have been produced in all of the stage types illustrated in Figure 3.1. Ibsen, on the other hand, wrote for a proscenium stage, but that does not prevent his scripts from being realized on an arena stage. The point here is simply that the various forms of the stage are all characterized by confinement. That in turn leads to the recognition that there are ultimately three distinct domains associated with stage space: onstage, offstage, and in the house. The fact that theatre depends on the act of presentation means that some space must serve for the presentation that is distinct from the space for an audience. Spectacle is somehow placed before spectator. This also means there must be some form of neutral space beyond our view—namely, offstage. From time immemorial, there has always been some form of "tiring-house" or "skene" or "wing space." Actors must come onto stage from somewhere and exit offstage to somewhere. For that they need a neutral space beyond our view. We may not see it, but we are aware of it, willing as we usually are to anticipate further arrivals and departures. If the motif of drama lies in the encounter, as argued earlier, this neutral space is very important. In the course of action, it may even assume character or exert force on the characters because offstage readily becomes an extension of the fictional domain of the play. Offstage takes on qualities of its own by virtue not only of providing for the confinement of the stage space itself but also by providing a virtual world beyond our view. Characters, events and sounds may emanate out of that world beyond and affect the characters set before our eyes.

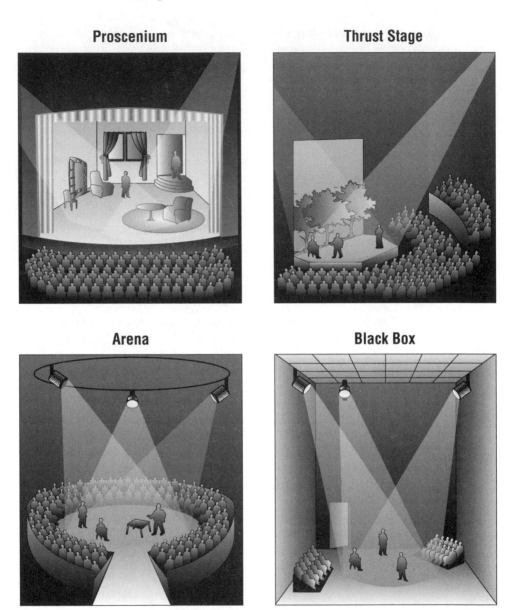

Proscenium

Thrust Stage

Arena

Black Box

FIGURE 3.1   Graphic representations of proscenium, thrust, arena, and black box stages.

Presentationalism versus Representationalism

In the second chapter, drama was described as being double edged because of its reliance on pretense. The actual activity the performers conduct among themselves on stage is accompanied by imagined activity transpiring among characters in their world. That in turn means that a play must rely on what is actually presented as well as what is represented as a fictional world. Some scripts throw more emphasis on the act of theatre, others on creating and sustaining the illusion of a life being lived. These are the two extremes. One is **presentationalism,** emphasizing the act of presentation, and the other is **representationalism,** emphasizing the representing of a life through illusion. Because the drama is a deliberate mixture of actual performance and imagined activity, it can never be purely presentational nor purely representational. The first would be direct performance with no hint of a fictional life, and the second would lack any sense of spectacle or interest.

Some scripts, however, do call for a more complete representation of life than others. These tend toward naturalism or at least realism. They purport to show us people living their lives in their own rooms, oblivious of anyone watching. Such a play suppresses the act of presentation, but it cannot eliminate it. The fact that it must incorporate the convention of the fourth wall confirms this truth. Somehow the play must open itself to the audience and engage its interest. Thus, it must incorporate some degree of presentationalism. As an acknowledgment of this condition, actor training always involves special work on "kisses, fights, and falls" for the very good reason that such activities cannot be done exactly as they are in real life. They must be carefully arranged, even choreographed, for presentation.

Other scripts demand a frank acknowledgment of the stage as a platform for presentation. The actors speak directly to us and the setting may even be bare, but the play engages our imagination to create a virtual existence for its characters. Such plays, then, carry a degree of representationalism. To do so, they also resort to convention in order for this to happen. In place of the fourth wall, the conventions used are appeals to the imagination. We are asked to translate what we see happening literally on stage into what is happening among the characters in their own world. We have seen this in connection with the Shakespearean soliloquy, wherein an actor stands and talks while we imagine a character wrestling with and within his mind. In fact, the following is Shakespeare's statement on the conditions called for in the presentational mode. This is the prologue to *Henry V,* in which the chorus challenges us to meet the terms of the play, purporting to show us great kingdoms, and asks us to pardon the lowly actors, those "flat unraised spirits that have dared"

> On this unworthy scaffold to bring forth
> So great an object: can this cockpit hold
> The vasty fields of France? Or may we cram
> Within this wooden O the very casques
> That did affright the air at Agincourt?
> O, pardon! Since a crooked figure may
> Attest in little place a million;
> And let us, ciphers to this great accompt,
> On your imaginary forces work.
> Suppose within the girdle of these walls
> Are now confined two mighty monarchies,
> Whose high upreared and abutting fronts
> The perilous narrow ocean parts asunder;

> Piece out our imperfections with your thoughts;
> Into a thousand parts divide one man,
> And make imaginary puissance;
> Think, when we talk of horses, that you see them
> Printing their proud hooves i' the receiving earth;
> For 'tis your thoughts that now must deck our kings,
> Carry them here and there; jumping o'er times,
> Turning the accomplishment of many years
> Into an hour glass . . .

This is an eloquent appeal to the audience to engage with the actors on stage and collaborate with them in creating out of that bare platform and the behavior of that motley crew great kingdoms, castles, throne rooms, and battlefields, none of which are literally there.

We have dealt with this matter before in connection with the nature of an audience's involvement in a play. In fact, Chapter 2 provides two sharply contrasting samples: Dario Fo's *Isabella, Three Sailing Ships and a Con Man*, a highly presentational play, and Anton Chekhov's *The Three Sisters*, a representational play (see pp. 29–30). What should be clear now is that a script must provide for the audience. What we call conventions are essentially agreements struck with the audience for any given play. They aid us in making the jump from witnessing the actual performance of actors to imagining the virtual activity of characters. A play carries with it the terms on which we will engage with it. In a script, those terms usually become clear very early, although rarely as explicitly as the chorus presented them in the example from *Henry V*, and we have to be alert to them if we are to analyze the piece. The terms will indicate where in the spectrum between the presentational and the representational modes the play will fall, but also specific understandings pertinent to the experience of that particular play.

Fixed, Fluid, and Floating Stages

The fact that the stage is in one way or another a confined space means that it carries a considerable restriction for the playwright, one that the screenwriter does not have to face with anything like the same rigor, for a camera can take the viewer anywhere in the fictional world of a movie. In the theatre, the action must reside on stage. Like all restrictions, however, this one challenges the creative energies. The playwright can take advantage of the confinement in a number of ways.

First, the playwright can take the confines of the stage as corresponding to the confines of the fictional space. This we might call the **fixed stage.** The limits of the stage space would then also be the limits of virtual space occupied by the characters. It is fixed in the sense that it remains the same throughout the play or at least throughout each act or scene; it does not vary. We are not asked to suppose that we are in one place at one moment and in an entirely different place the next moment. We are not "carried here and there" and there is no "jumping o'er time." The characters are caught in this space. Although they may exit, the place remains the same.

If they are to reappear, they must reenter through the same place they left through. Realism virtually demands a fixed stage. If the effort is to create the sensation of seeing characters live as they might be observed in real life, then they must occupy a space that is recognizable, detailed, and fixed, typically a room. Classical plays of the Greek theatre tended toward the fixed stage, the action represented often taking place in front of a palace or a temple. The same is true of neoclassical drama, in the plays of Molière or Racine. Moreover, it reappears in modern nonrealistic plays, such as the absurdist pieces of Beckett and Ionesco, both of whom use the confines of the stage for metaphysical or symbolic purposes. There is a long and varied tradition associated with the fixed stage.

Another tradition, one fully contrary to the fixed stage, is the **fluid stage.** Although the fluid stage maintains the confines of the stage for the duration of a segment of action, it may jump to another place and time on a moment's notice. It can carry us "here and there," as it were. We may be for a time in front of Brabantio's house, as we are at the outset of *Othello*, and soon after in the streets of Venice, and soon after that in the Venetian Senate chamber, and still later at the port of the island of Cyprus. In any one of these instances, the confines of the stage space are respected, but we willingly accept that after a time we may be somewhere else. This bothered the neoclassicists, including Voltaire and others. They argued, for example, that it is unreasonable to suppose we have shifted scenes from Venice to Cyprus when we have ourselves not moved an inch from our seats. Such an attitude fails to take into account the audience's capacity to collaborate imaginatively in the creation of the world of the play. We gladly accept that we have changed locale, or even that days, months, or years have elapsed, so long as it carries us into new facets of the story. Naturally, this sort of fluid stage is closely associated with the Elizabethan theatre, but also with the commedia dell'arte in Italy and earlier with the medieval theatre. It endures today in the work of epic playwrights such as Bertolt Brecht, Dario Fo, Caryl Churchill, Edward Bond, and Tony Kushner.

In between these two varieties is a middle ground, what we call the **floating stage.** This is not as rigid as the fixed stage, for it allows us to move imaginatively from place to place, but these places are themselves within some larger confinement. It is floating in the sense that it is by no means anchored to one specific locale but moves about from one corner to another within the same closed world. This is the case, for example, in Thornton Wilder's *Our Town*. We spend the entire play imaginatively in Grovers Corners, New Hampshire, but we also accept that we may simultaneously be at the homes of two families, as Emily and George talk across from stepladder to stepladder (from one bedroom window to another), at another moment in a soda fountain, at another at the breakfast table, or at another on the street. Likewise, in Friedrich Dürrenmatt's *The Visit*, all of which takes place in the town of Güllen, we may at one moment be at the train station, another at the hotel, another in a store, or another at the town hall, but we are also always in Güllen. The floating stage incorporates several places within a general environment. This is sometimes the case when we are witnessing the visions, hallucinations, or memories of a character, as in the case of Jerome Lawrence and Robert E. Lee's *The Night Thoreau Spent in Jail*, or Milan Stitt's *The Runner Stumbles*, or Peter Luke's *Hadrian VII*.

Concentrated versus Comprehensive Dramaturgy

Emanating from these three kinds of stages or confined spaces are two distinct ways of structuring a play, or dramaturgy. **Concentrated dramaturgy** makes use of a tight, compact action, picking it up near the moment of crisis and developing tension out of the urgency it engenders. It employs a "late point of attack," meaning that much of the story has already occurred and we attack it, as it were, late in its development. Such a structure tends to maintain a cause-to-effect progression, building a strong sense of impending reversals that cause an intense anticipation in the audience. Naturally, this structure tends to rely on a single setting and on action that transpires in more or less the same amount of fictional time as real time. The so-called unities of time and place are natural to concentrated dramaturgy. Because of the compactness of this structure, much tension can develop out of the contrast between present and past, between the way things are now and the way they once were, between "now" and "then." For that matter, contrasts between the present and an ominous or threatening future may create a binding tension. By the same token, concentrated dramaturgy is likely to develop tension between the space of the action and the virtual world beyond our view, between "here" and "there," as it were. Certain periods in theatre history have favored concentrated dramaturgy: the Greeks of the fifth century B.C., the neoclassicists of the seventeenth century, and the realists of the late nineteenth and twentieth centuries. We associate it with the work of Sophocles, Racine, Molière, Ibsen, and Arthur Miller. They all favor concentrated dramaturgy for various reasons and in different styles, but they nevertheless attain a similar effect through the strong urgency and compact economy that this tight structure affords them.

The second approach to play structure is **comprehensive dramaturgy.** With the help of the audience's imagination, the stage space assumes a certain elasticity, becoming a fluid stage capable of representing multiple realms and times. This allows much of the natural story line to be shown and allows for an early point of attack. The plot tends to be episodic. This does not necessarily mean a loss of dramatic effect. Tension now tends to be shaped by the juxtaposition of one episode with another. Cause to effect may not be as important as ironic or emotional contrasts between one scene and the preceding one, as well as the one following. Comprehensive dramaturgy encourages a great sweep of action involving a whole society and perhaps a cavalcade of years. Contrasts are still possible between the immediate world before our eyes and the implicit virtual world beyond. After all, the stage remains a confined space. Tension is also more apt to develop between what we are literally witnessing with our eyes and ears and what we experience in our imagination. This is the case, for example, with a Shakespearean soliloquy: We see an actor alone on stage talking, but we imagine him thinking. This type of structuring naturally tends toward the presentational mode and the fluid stage. It too was favored in certain periods of theatre history: the Elizabethan theatre, the Spanish golden age, and epic theatre in the twentieth century. We associate it with the work of such playwrights as William Shakespeare, Ben Jonson, Lope de Vega, Pedro Calderón, Bertolt Brecht, Peter Weiss, Dario Fo, and others.

Theatre of Illusion versus
Theatre of Communion

The contrast between these two ways of play structuring is analogous to the contrast between representational and presentational modes of drama. The concentrated structure encourages the representational mode, and the comprehensive encourages the presentational mode. They are not absolute parallels, however: It is possible to have a concentrated presentational play, for example. Several plays out of the Greek theatre are in this vein: *Oedipus Rex* is both concentrated and presentational. Nevertheless, there is an analogous pattern here. We may also see another contrast working analogously: the contrast between the theatre of illusion and that of communion. These are distinguished by how the play engages the audience.

In the case of the **theatre of illusion,** the audience experiences the sensation of peering into another world beyond its own. Playgoers are witnessing an illusion and, when it is well done, they relish the transporting richness of the experience. This variety of theatre was very much a part of the Renaissance in Italy, from the sixteenth century on, even into the nineteenth century. The creation then of false-perspective scenery that gave the audience the illusion of tremendous depth, changeable wings and drops that could take us to new locales at a moment's notice, and the proscenium arch to conceal the illusion-making machinery, were all devices to suggest a vivid other world beyond the one we occupy in the theatre house. A similar experience attended on the work of the naturalists and realists at the end of the nineteenth century and beginning of the twentieth. The effort here entailed an even more complete illusion, reinforced by the convention of the fourth wall. That convention gives the audience the distinct impression that it is looking through an invisible wall to watch a life being lived beyond it by characters unaware of being observed. In such instances, every effort is made to provide the detail, the look, and the feel of a real room. The illusion of a distinct reality appears also in symbolism and expressionism, which seek to create the sensation of a dream encased in the stage space beyond a "mystic gulf" (as Richard Wagner called it) separating the illusion from the darkened domain of the theatre house. Certainly, we can experience great pleasure in savoring these rich illusions.

This tendency is in some measure parallel to the representational mode and to concentrated dramaturgy. It naturally strives to suppress our awareness of the act of presentation and our own presence in the theatre. It also encourages the use of a closed and confined stage, which naturally favors concentrated dramaturgy. But again the analogy is not quite complete, for it is possible for the illusion to shift, especially in the current theatre with the use of changing lights, projections, and computer-generated images that allow us to jump over time in the spirit of comprehensive dramaturgy. That certainly is the case with such plays as August Strindberg's *The Dream Play* or Georg Kaiser's *From Morn to Midnight.* Moreover, playwrights can merge the illusion on stage with some form of awareness of the audience's presence, which appears in many examples of grand opera, elaborate musicals such as *Cats* or *Phantom of the Opera*, and even some plays out of the theatre of the absurd, such as Samuel Beckett's *Waiting for Godot* or Tom Stoppard's

Rosencrantz and Guildenstern Are Dead. These plays use illusion but with a spirit of presentationalism mixed in.

At the opposite end of the spectrum, the **theatre of communion** acknowledges the audience's presence, sharing the creation of the virtual lives of the characters with the audience. It plays on the audience's imagination to create entire worlds that are not literally represented on stage. In other words, the audience has the pleasure of collaborating with the actors in conjuring the characters and the places they occupy. This is not to say that there is no illusion operating in the theatre of communion, only that the illusion emerges from appeals to the audience's imagination, rather than being provided through lights, properties, and scenery. Inasmuch as this form of theatre plays on the act of performance and the presence of the audience, it naturally tends toward the presentational. Moreover, relying as it does on imagination, it has the capacity to move from place to place and time to time with relative ease and therefore favors comprehensive dramaturgy. Prime examples come from the Elizabethan theatre with such plays as Shakespeare's *King Lear* or *Henry V* and Ben Jonson's *Bartholomew Fair,* from the Spanish golden age with such plays as Lope de Vega's *The Sheep Well* and Calderón's *Life Is a Dream,* and from the contemporary theatre with such plays as Bertolt Brecht's *The Caucasian Chalk Circle,* Arthur Kopit's *Indians,* and Tony Kushner's *Angels in America.*

Here we have three sets of polarities: representational versus presentational, concentrated versus comprehensive, and illusion versus communion. All of them derive from the mutual presence of a virtual, fictional existence (characters living within their world) and an actual platform or performance space (upon which actors move and talk). All this is also closely related to the contrary impulses of empathy (engaging with the virtual world) and aesthetic distance (viewing the play as a contrivance) that together establish willing suspension of disbelief. For purposes of analysis, these are useful, as we shall now see, in recognizing one of the basic sources of tension to engage an audience—the tension between the actual and the virtual. This tension can be manipulated by a playwright in innumerable ways. In the act of composing a play script, the playwright must somehow come to terms with how the play is to open itself to the audience. The playwright must calculate and design the audience's role in the experience of the intended play. Moreover, the audience's role is fundamental to how we analyze the play in its script format. Although we may not be privileged to witness the play, the terms on which the play is to work in performance are integral to the script and thus accessible to analysis. How this is so we shall now explore.

Fundamental Sources of Tension in Space

We should now be able to catalog basic sources that a playwright can tap to create the essential tension of a play. The first of the many sources of tension (and interest) derives from the polarity of spectacle and spectator. This occurs at the very outset of a play. The moment the lights come up on stage, we are riveted to the action about to transpire there. This will be the finest moment in a bad play. A good play, however, will play on that tension and enhance it by introducing other, more varied tensions. A graphic representation of the most basic of tensions is shown in Figure 3.2.

In this diagram, the space within the circle belongs to the play itself. Inasmuch as a play depends on its context, set apart in some way from other space, that other space, offstage and in the audience, actually figures in the design of the play. Note that a play occupies three distinct realms: onstage, offstage, and auditorium. The very act of presentation sets up an initial polarity between spectacle and spectator. We may very quickly be aware of the offstage space as we anticipate the arrival of other actors. Almost at once there are tensions operating between the stage action and the audience and between onstage and offstage. This constitutes the actual, physical arrangement of the theatre event, even if it is purely a presentation, such as a lion tamer's performance or a tightrope walk. If we add to the mix the mutual presence of a virtual or imagined existence, new sources of tension become available.

A play occupies not only three realms (onstage, offstage, auditorium) but also three levels on which we experience the play: performance, virtual life, and inner life. Tension arises often between the first two levels. While we watch flesh-and-blood human beings performing on the stage before our eyes, enjoying their movements, gestures, facial expressions, and words, we are also mindful of the presence of the virtual world, imagined activities transpiring among characters in a world of their own. Marcel Marceau on his tightrope adds this virtual dimension to the experience that is not there in a real tightrope walk. Here too is a possible source of tension. It can emerge from the disparity between what is literally transpiring among the performers and what their characters are doing. By necessity there is

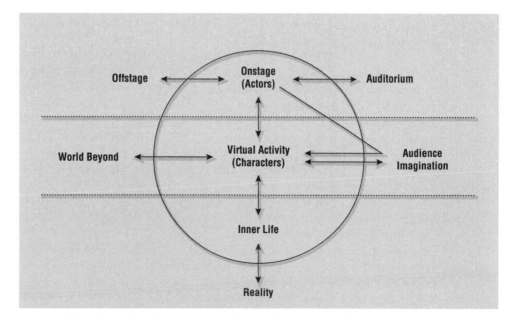

FIGURE 3.2 A graphic representation of dramatic tension.

always some disparity because the stage cannot duplicate life, but it is possible to play up the disparity and create a tension by doing so. This is the case in many presentational, comprehensive, communion plays, for they elicit from the audience's imagination a richer, fuller fictional world than the sparse or even bare stage could ever represent. The Isabella–Christopher Columbus play of Dario Fo is a case in point and so is Bertolt Brecht's *The Good Woman of Setzuan.*

What is also true is that the virtual counterpart of the offstage domain, the world beyond, can become a powerful source of tension. If there were somehow a virtual world before our eyes, it would have a natural extension beyond the stage's confines. Some characters may exist out there. We may never see them, and yet they can assume a force of their own. This is the case in such plays as Tennessee Williams's *The Glass Menagerie* (the father who "fell in love with long distances"), Harold Pinter's man at the other end of the dumb waiter in *The Dumb Waiter,* and Samuel Beckett's *Waiting for Godot.* Not only unseen characters but also unseen places can exert power over the characters, such as Moscow in *The Three Sisters* and Belle Reve in *A Streetcar Named Desire.* "Here versus there" can be a vivid tension operating in a play.

This contrast can be, and often is, enhanced by drawing a sharp distinction between spaces that are adjacent to the space the characters occupy and those that are far away. In some plays, we become very aware of what is happening in, say, the next room. Someone may be lurking just outside the house. We do not need to see the person to sense the tension. It might be more powerful if we do not. Meanwhile, there may be many references to a remote place that holds some significance for the characters. Moscow in *The Three Sisters* is such a place, and it is set in contrast to nearby sounds that tend to increase as the play progresses, sounds of the wind in act 2, the fire and fire engines in act 3, and the gunshot in act 4. While the sisters look to the remote world they once knew in Moscow, life passes by just outside and snatches their dreams.

As soon as a virtual existence emerges and characters begin to come to life, a third level develops for the audience. Watching these characters encounter the circumstances of their lives, the audience may well begin to sense their mental and emotional lives. A vicarious experience then accompanies the aesthetic experience, taking us to the third level of a play's life. Again, it is possible for a playwright to tap this third level as a source of tension. There may well be some disparity, incongruity, or contrast between what a character is doing and his or her mind-set while doing it. This of course is the case with many realistic playwrights. They attempt to blur the distinction between the actual activity of actors and the imagined activity of characters and in doing so may manage to create an intense and sometimes poignant disparity between activity and inner life. We have seen this in the example from Chekhov's *The Three Sisters.*

When the play is in full progress, and certainly at the moment of its final curtain, the audience naturally draws parallels and correspondences between the life of the play and life itself. If the play is genuinely moving and engaging, there is apt to be a powerful interaction between the lives of its characters and the lives that its audience knows. So it is that the audience's sense of reality standing outside the play is tapped and engaged on that third level. Although probably none of us has occupied a position of royal power and suffered its loss, we can all relate to King Lear, for on some analogous level we know his experience. Or, to take a more mundane example, we may never have lived in Moscow, but we may well know the feeling of separation from a time and place that constitutes a nostalgic loss, a feeling keenly felt by Chekhov's three sisters. Or, perhaps still more mundane but equally powerful, the sense of losing a great opportunity to someone quicker and more alert provokes the junk dealer, Don, in David Mamet's *American Buffalo*, into an outrageous robbery scheme, one that few of us would consider, and yet we can still share in his provocation. One of the paradoxes of the drama is that it can achieve "universality," a genuine meaningfulness, only through the particular. It is the details that convince us of lives being lived by the characters; once convinced, we can relate to them as fellow human beings. All this illustrates still another paradox: A play separates itself from actuality in order to reflect on reality. This is Langer's opacity–transparency principle discussed in Chapter 2.

Further Sources of Tension

The space of the stage itself may well be manipulated to produce some degree of tension. When the space contains two or more distinct realms, the audience becomes sensitive to the interplay of action taking place among them. The Elizabethan stage was architecturally a number of distinct realms: the discovery space, the inner above, the windows and doors, the space below the stage, and even the "heavens" over the stage could all be juxtaposed to create interest and variety. Hamlet meets Ophelia on the forestage while in the back discovery space Claudius and Polonius have hidden themselves to eavesdrop. Romeo below, supposedly in the garden, woos Juliet above on the inner above, her balcony. Mephistopheles creeps up out of smoke from the trap in the floor of the stage in Christopher Marlowe's *Dr. Faustus*. All of these are examples of uses made of the architectural features of the playhouse. Modern plays have sometimes characterized the stage space as malleable, its space representing now one place, now another. An interesting instance of this is Arthur Kopit's *Indians*, which ostensibly presents the space of a Wild West show, but the space transforms readily into many different locales as the story demands.

We might assume that realistic plays do not have such an option because, after all, they tend simply to represent rooms. Playwrights can exercise the option by dividing the room into areas. This is the case in the example given previously of the set for the first act of *The Three Sisters*, in which the room consists of a parlor area in the foreground and a dining alcove upstage of it. As we have seen, the action in the latter can undercut the action in the former, as it does in the opening scene when the military gentlemen are at the dining table and the three sisters in the parlor area (see pp. 29–30). *Hedda Gabler* also uses an alcove area set apart from a sitting room, and that is the area in which the crucial moment occurs when the main character shoots herself. Plays such as Eugene O'Neill's *Desire under the Elms* and Arthur Miller's *Death of a Salesman* take this idea a step further and portray the several rooms of a house, allowing for the juxtaposition of action in one room with that in another to produce some form of tension. Thus Abby and Eben sense each other through the wall separating their rooms in O'Neill's play. We see the house as a cutaway, making visible their two rooms, the kitchen, and ultimately the sitting room. Spatially the scenery reflects the tension that arises out of their desire for each another, which they must suppress because of Cabot, Eben's father and Abby's new husband, who resides out in the yard or in the kitchen. When they can no longer contain themselves, they burst into the sitting room that had been closed up since Eben's mother's death. Miller's play also uses a cutaway view of the house, showing the kitchen, master bedroom, and upstairs bedroom. *Death of a Salesman* is a play about the faltering mind of Willy Loman, who is watched over by his wife Linda and his sons, Biff and Happy. The sons in their bedroom listen to the ravings of Willy in the kitchen, and Willy occasionally emerges in the yard to engage in conversation with Uncle Ben, a figment of his imagination.

Still another way in which stage space can contribute tension by being split appears in the convention of the "simultaneous set." This idea goes back at least as far as the Middle Ages, when a typical staging practice was to line up a series of "mansions," scenic representations of the locales that figure in the action of the play. They appear adjacent to one another, but in fact stand for places that may be far distant from one another: heaven, the Garden of Eden, Mount Ararat, Bethlehem, Pontius Pilate's palace, and Calvary, for example, all gathered together on the same stage. The same idea appears in many plays of our own time. The stage space can contain representations of a number of places that we accept as being at some distance from one another. Lanford Wilson's *The Rimers of Eldridge* uses different parts of the stage to suggest different places around the town of Eldridge. Tennessee Williams presents three disparate places, a sitting room, a city park monument, and a doctor's office, in his *Summer and Smoke.* A truly remarkable and inventive use of stage space appears in Tom Stoppard's *Arcadia.* All of the action takes place in the same room, but it is action sometimes belonging to 1809 and sometimes belonging to the present day, and gradually the characters from the earlier time begin to merge in that room with the characters of our time, unaware of one another and yet there in the same space. Another novel use of space appears in Maria Irene Fornes's *Fefu and Her Friends,* which sets the first scene in one room shared by the entire audience, which then splits into four different audiences visiting four different rooms witnessing the action in each by turns until they reassemble in the room where they started.

Tensions Deriving from Temporal Isolation

The context of a play's action is not only confined to stage space but it is also shaped by the virtual past of the characters. Just as there are boundaries to the space a play occupies, so are there limits to its time. A play starts at a certain moment in its natural story line and it ends at another. Thus there is always the potential for tension to emerge out of the contrast between the present in the characters' lives and their past experience. Inasmuch as this is a matter of establishing the context for the play's action, it is fixed and unchanging. These past events are over and done with. But they can be a powerful source of tension as the memory of them and their effects continue to exert a force on the characters. They create the conditions governing the present lives of the characters. In that sense, they are something akin to spatial tensions. So just as we have seen potential tension in the contrast between "in here" and "out there," we may also see it in the contrast between "now" and "then."

This tension is likely to be much stronger in the instance of concentrated dramaturgy for the very good reason that it tends to cut off much more of the natural story line. Whenever this tension is tapped, revelations about the past may well occur throughout the action of the play, and each one has the capacity to affect the course of that action. One of the most tightly constructed plays of all time is *Oedipus Rex,* in which Oedipus's search for the murderer of Laius takes us further and further into the past. Each discovery brings us closer to the ironic recognition that the man Oedipus seeks is himself. Comprehensive dramaturgy, despite its open structure, is still capable of creating tension out of temporal isolation. Consider, for example, the events that precede the opening of *Hamlet.* Two months ago, Hamlet Senior died; young Hamlet came home from Wittenberg for the funeral; Hamlet senior's brother, Claudius, seized the throne rightfully Hamlet's, and one month ago he married his sister-in-law, the widow Gertrude; and the last two nights, the ghost of Old Hamlet was seen to walk on the ramparts of the castle of Elsinore. All of these events function as factors weighing down Hamlet's spirit. Together they launch Hamlet's powerful, intense effort to resolve both the inner, personal turmoil he suffers and the outward, public rottenness of the state of Denmark.

Just as far away places may be set against adjacent spaces, so may the remote past be contrasted with the immediate past. Things may have happened years ago that still affect the characters now. Previous events have produced conditions with which characters are still struggling. Plays often play off such backgrounds. Meanwhile, there are always some events in the very recent past that feed into the action, prompting more action. The remote past may be in sharp contrast to the immediate past, perhaps by seeming now idyllic and pleasant, whereas the recent events are disturbing and unsettling. Blanche DuBois, for example, has just been run out of Meridian, but long ago she lived a gracious life at the Belle Reve plantation. Or it is possible that the past contains an event so horrible that the characters refuse to deal with it until recent events force them to do so, as in the case of Sam Shepard's *Buried Child,* wherein incest and murder committed long ago force their way into the present moment, first by way of an inexplicable stand of corn that has suddenly cropped up out back, and then by way of the unearthed corpse.

The future implied in a play's action can also contribute tension. We may know about the future in a way that the characters do not. Thus it is not unusual for a degree of ironic tension to develop because of this disparity. Sophocles' contemporaries surely knew that the murderer Oedipus sought was himself. Because *Hamlet* is a recognized type of drama, the revenge tragedy, we expect to see that revenge pursued and probably accomplished, although at a terrible cost. Some plays begin with the culminating scene and then step back in time to trace the path that characters followed to bring them to that point. Both James Baldwin's *Blues for Mr. Charlie* and Charles Fuller's *A Soldier's Story* begin with murder scenes and then trace the events that led up to them. An interesting variation on this is Tom

Stoppard's *Arcadia*, which, as mentioned earlier, takes place in the same room in two different time periods. As the characters in the present time discover along with the audience more about the characters out of the past, we come to see the scenes out of the past, knowing what the future holds for those characters. That double vision produces a palpable tension. Still another interesting variation on this sort of tension is found in Michael Frayne's *Copenhagen*, a play set in some place beyond the grave as the characters try to piece together their lives and relationships on earth. The characters are Nils Bohr, his wife, Margrethe, and Walter Heisenberg. Because the two men are famous physicists, Bohr for his contributions to the U.S. development of the atomic bomb in the midst of World War II and Heisenberg for working toward that same end for the Nazis, we find a particular fascination in the drama deriving from our knowledge of how the war turned out. The fact that it might have turned out otherwise gives the play a special power. Again, all of these tensions are rendered possible by the necessary isolation of the time span of the play's action.

Tensions among Characters

Finally, we should recognize contextual tensions that reside among the characters of a play. Much more is said on this score in the next chapter, which deals with temporal sources of tension usually emerging as conflict. For the time being, however, we will concentrate on provocative disparities between one character and another or between one group of characters and another. Such disparities can at the very least spark interest and vivify personalities; sometimes they develop into outright conflict. In either case, they often form patterns meaningful to the play as a whole.

Among the first impressions we glean of a play we are about to see or a script we are about to read come from the title and the cast of characters. Both can be revealing. The title sometimes suggests tensions that will develop. Examples include *Mother Courage* (which suggests a tension between protective motherhood and bravery), *The Glass Menagerie* (which suggests a contrast between the delicate and the animalistic), and *Accidental Death of an Anarchist* (which implies both mayhem and death). The cast of characters is usually more enlightening. Quite often we can recognize groupings of characters that might produce tension. The cast for *Six Characters in Search of an Author* by Luigi Pirandello consists of persons identified by their family relationships (these are the characters searching for the author: Father, Mother, Stepdaughter, Son) and others identified by their duties in the theatrical company (Director, Prompter, Leading Man, Leading Lady). The contrast suggests some tension growing out of the interaction between the two groups. Henrik Ibsen's *A Doll's House* provides another illustration; its cast consists on the one hand of Torvald Helmer and his wife Nora, their small children, and members of the household staff, and on the other hand three apparent outsiders to the family: Dr. Rank, Mrs. Linde, and Nils Krogstad, a bank clerk. We might expect that these outsiders will have some impact on the marriage and the family, and indeed they do. And then of course there is a clear illustration in *Romeo and Juliet*, in which some characters are Montagues and others Capulets.

One more source of tension can arise when characters are at odds with their circumstances. We have seen this in the list detailed earlier of the factors burdening Hamlet's spirit at the beginning of the play, to which we soon add the call for revenge issued by the ghost of his murdered father. At the outset of any play, factors are laid out for the characters, especially the protagonist, to deal with. Mme. Ranevskaya in Chekhov's *The Cherry Orchard* must deal with the fact that her cherry orchard and entire estate is scheduled to be auctioned off. Don, in David Mamet's *American Buffalo,* is uncomfortable about the price he got for the nickel he sold in his junk shop. Everybody is at odds with his or her sexuality in Caryl Churchill's *Cloud 9.* We might say that the business of playwriting consists of putting characters in uncomfortable positions much as a biologist tests microscopic organisms by placing them in irritating cultures. Out of this discomfort dramatic action arises. As soon as it does, we are entering into the temporal dimension of drama.

The mention of *Cloud 9* and its curious device of role-playing suggests one last source of contextual tension. In that play, actors play one role in act 1 and another role in act 2, which takes place a hundred years after act 1 even though the characters have aged only twenty-five years. The actors play across gender and racial lines, a man playing a woman, a white man playing a black man, even a stuffed doll playing a child. This is an extreme example of the tension that plays naturally assume by virtue of having to be enacted. The mutual presence of actual actor and virtual character is one of the charms of theatre. This is not, however, always programmatic or evident in scripts. It is a factor in certain historical periods, such as Elizabethan drama and Japanese Kabuki, both of which made deliberate use of boys or very young men to play all female roles. It also shows up in certain metatheatrical or self-referential ways, as in the case of Jean Anouilh's *Ring Round the Moon,* in which twins are played by the same actor, which means they can never meet, or in the case of Heiner Müller's *Hamletmachine,* in which the actor deliberately sets himself apart from the role he is playing (Hamlet) to become himself tearing the picture of the playwright and later to become Ophelia. Still another interesting variation on this theme is the way in which actors relate to roles in Edward Albee's *Three Tall Women:* In act 1 they are three distinct women, but in act 2 they have all merged into one woman at different times in her past life, as she (now represented as a mannequin stretched out in bed) is dying. The actor–character tension is always there and sometimes tapped for dramatic effect.

The Full Array of Potential Tensions

We have now cataloged the many places we might discover contrasts, disparities, or incongruities in a play. What we are seeking are the patterns that characterize these potential tensions. It should be reassuring to realize that no worthy play will tap *all* these sources. To do so would create an indecipherable pastiche. Locating the ones used can be instructive about the overall design and subject matter of the play. Furthermore, patterns are apt to emerge from the way tensions are shaped and made to relate to one another. Then it remains to see how they play into the dramatic action itself.

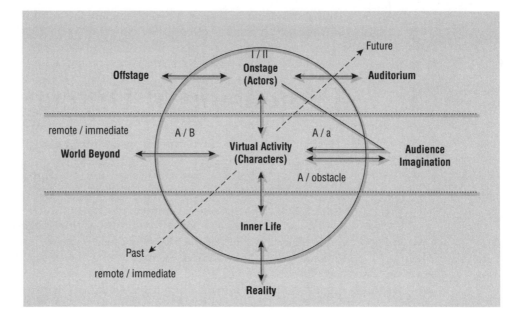

FIGURE 3.3   Complex representation of dramatic tension.

By way of review, Figure 3.3 is a new and improved diagram of these many sources, enlarging on the diagram seen in Figure 3.2. The chart illustrates the following list of tensions:

1. Neutral offstage ground versus actual onstage activity of the performers versus the presence of the audience in the house
2. World beyond versus the virtual activity of the characters versus the collective imagination of the audience
3. The immediate world beyond versus the remote world
4. The virtual activity of the characters versus the activity of their inner lives
5. The past versus the present versus the future
6. The immediate past versus the remote past
7. One part of the stage (I) versus another part (II)
8. One character (A) versus another or group of others (B)
9. Character versus circumstance or obstacle
10. Character versus actor (A/a)
11. The whole of the play versus the outside world and our sense of reality

Bear in mind that the word *tension* does not denote outright conflict or contradiction. Playwrights use sources of tension to create interest and focus the action of the play. Anywhere or anyone who might develop a contrast, disparity, or incongruity can enhance the dramatic experience. Playwrights do this to invest their work with power and meaning. Analysts in their turn need to explore where and how the tensions are shaped. This will be different for every play.

CHAPTER

4

The Temporal Dimension of Drama

The previous chapter concentrated on the contextual dimension of drama. The context in which the action takes place includes the literal space the actors occupy (the stage), as well as the imagined world the characters live in. It also includes how the present action is set off from the past and from the implied future. In other words, a play develops many of its effects from the "nesting" of its action. We see the action in context. Usually this context carries the potential for many tensions. It then remains for the forward movement of the action to play on that potential, to elaborate its tensions. So now it is time to turn to action as it transpires in time. This, of course, is the temporal dimension of drama.

The very term "action" implies change and it provokes anticipation. Seated in a theatre, we watch the lights in the house fade and the stage lights come up. This is always a delicious moment. We are about to meet a group of people and the world they inhabit. We are alert to everything that makes up the initial impression: the set, the lights, the actors, their costumes . . . everything. We want to learn about these characters, know who they are, where they live, how they relate to one another, what they want . . . again, everything. This is theatre—it is an exciting moment. In the case of a bad play, it may be the only exciting moment. A good play will seize on this natural curiosity and play on it to develop a powerful momentum that keeps us with the play until the end. It is as though we say to ourselves, "All right, this is the world of the play and these are its people; now what?" Four questions make up a test for the structure of a play in the making, four questions prod the imagination of the playwright: (1) What if? (2) Why now? (3) Why here? and (4) So what? In other words, a play is structured on a given set of conditions (What if?) set in a particular moment (Why now?) and in a particular place (Why here?). Out of this must grow the action (So what?). This last question has a double meaning: It refers to what grows out of the given circumstances and to whether it matters at all.

Progression in Time

We might first look at a play's progression in time as an interaction, again, between the stage activity and the audience's perception of it. In *The Elements of Drama*, J. L. Styan presents a chart of a play's movement through time. Liberally adapting this chart to our purposes, it can serve as a counterpart to the chart in Chapter 3 of theatrical space. Again, we are dealing with dramatic action on the same three levels of actual activity, virtual activity, and inner life. Composing a play script, a play-wright seeks ways of making the characters and their world fully palpable to an audience. In the course of rehearsal, actors, in collaboration with the director, test their expressive instruments of body and voice to convey to an audience both the imagined worlds of the characters and the inner workings of their minds. Engaging with the audience's faculties of imagination and histrionic sensibility, the play taps our sense of reality and rounds out and completes itself with a total effect by the time it comes to an end. Each activity presented on stage, coupled with the previous one and set in its context, moves on to a new activity, and together they shape the audience's response. The physical activity accumulates to the point of shaping an impression of imagined activity, and that activity creates in us an effect. By the end of the play, these effects have accumulated to the point at which, as demonstrated in Figure 4.1, we sense the play's reflection of reality, the play's total effect.

By analogy, all of this is akin to watching a person fill a kettle with water, turn on the stove, and place the kettle on the heat, all of which adds up to a person boiling water. Or we might see a person lay out a shirt, select a button, place it on the shirt, unroll a length of thread, feed the thread through the eye of a needle, tie a knot at the end of the thread, push the needle through a hole in the button and into the material of the shirt, and we translate all of this into sewing a button on a shirt. The interaction of stage activity and audience perception is more complicated than this because it works on so many more levels, but these analogies provide a map to what happens as an audience attends a play.

For one thing, the process entails sensing not only the movement from activity to activity but also the context in which it resides. Our impressions derive from both the juxtaposition of one event with its predecessor and the surroundings of the event. The linkage between events is as important as the context. Moreover, the link is not just a matter of recognizing what is going on among the characters, but also how the action resonates within the context of their lives and ultimately with ours as well. Finally, in the case of a play, all these activities are bound together by some form of struggle that creates a driving force, a trajectory of action.

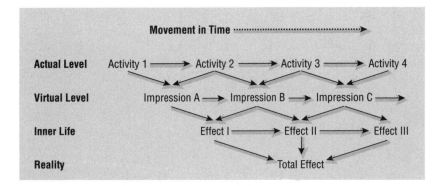

FIGURE 4.1   **A graphic representation of the temporal element of dramatic tension.**

Segmentation of Time: Formal and Organic

The spirit of struggle sparks the forward movement of any play. Without struggle there is no action. Most often the central character, the protagonist, carries the struggle. It is no accident that the word *drama* derives from a Greek word for "to do" and *protagonist* from the word for "contest." Doing, combating, struggling, contesting, conflicting—all these terms are kin to drama. The struggle may extend somewhere beyond or even center on any individual character, and may even reside within the audience caught up in the spectacle. As we have seen, there are many sources for tension. The point here is that plays take their structure from the spectacle of struggle, and that requires time.

A play typically begins when an event disturbs the natural balance of the characters' world. It throws them off their usual expectations sufficiently to cause them discomfort or distress, worry or concern. Things are not as they were. In good plays, this happens quickly. This disturbing event provokes action. This movement requires two factors: the conditions of the characters' lives, which may already have a disturbing element in it, and a sudden event. The condition in *Hamlet,* for example, is the recent death of old Hamlet and the marriage of his queen so soon afterward, and the disturbing event is the appearance of old Hamlet's ghost on the ramparts charging young Hamlet with accomplishing his revenge. The condition in *Oedipus* is the plague that has infected the city of Thebes, whereas the disturbing event is the report from the oracle that the plague will continue until the killer of the previous king is found and expelled from the city.

Once the condition is clear and the disturbance occurs, the characters seek at once to put things to rights. It is this struggle that constitutes the action of the play and might well be called the driving force of the play. Along the way, the force will encounter obstacles and opposing forces, which will force it into twists and turns to accomplish its goal. This spectacle of striving against all odds serves to bind together the events of the play to produce an arc of action that rounds out with either triumph or frustration. The state of things at the end of a play is rarely what it was at the beginning. This is true even of Samuel Beckett's *Waiting for Godot,* which ends with the characters hearing that Godot will not come today but will surely come tomorrow. The wait tomorrow will be different because of the wait today and the wait of yesterday, for that matter.

Remember Brunetière's definition of a play as "a spectacle of a will striving toward a goal and conscious of the means it employs"—an apt description. The arc of action can now be broken down into phases. First, however, it would be useful to examine ways in which time is broken down. The articulation of time produces meaningful segments. How this works is our first order of business in exploring the temporal dimension of drama.

Just as plays occupy confined space, so too do they occur within confined time. When we see a play begin, we have every right to expect it to end, and they all do, although sometimes rather later than we would wish. Play scripts often start with such phrases as "As the curtain rises" or "Lights up" and end with "The curtain falls" or "Blackout." Such indications also appear at moments when the action comes to the end of a scene or an act and a new scene or act begins. These are formal breaks, or **formal segments.** The action stops and starts by some device associated with the apparatus of theatre: curtains or lights. Even Shakespeare and his fellow Elizabethans, who did not use a proscenium curtain or artificial lights, used formal shifts occasioned by the exit of one set of characters and entrance of another set, speaking of their new surroundings (e.g., King Duncan's remark to his entourage on "arriving" at Dunsinane, Macbeth's castle: "This castle hath a pleasant seat"). Audiences relish change, not change for its own sake, but change that shifts focus, reveals new facets, builds anticipation, and enhances meaning. Nothing would be so irritating as to have a play go on and on without break, without new contexts or issues. What would be the point of enduring a play that constantly and meaninglessly starts and stops, episode after episode, with no sense of direction or purpose? Plays exist in segmented time, segmented in two fundamental ways: formally and organically. Formal segments are those we have just described: breaks that occur by the formal operation of the theatrical apparatus, acts and scenes that occasion a full stop in action.

Organic segments are more subtle, more difficult to define. Even so, we can sense them vividly as they occur, which is whenever a shift in tension occurs. Dramatic action grows from tension, one character working against another or against circumstance or against time itself. The tension is constantly shifting. New circumstances arise, new characters appear, time passes, motivations transform. These are changes inherent in the fictional world of the play and for that reason might be termed "organic." They emerge out of the very organism of the play. Film theorists speak of cinematic effects as being either "diegetic" or "nondiegetic." Those that are nondiegetic are associated with the mechanism of making a film: background music, fades or cross-fades, voice-over narration, blurring images or racking focus. Diegetic effects by contrast are those associated with the world of the film: the interaction of the characters and the sounds and sights that surround them. This is essentially the same distinction we are making between the formal and the organic in stage plays. Because film makes much fuller use of technology, machinery, electronic devices, and editing equipment, we are much more aware of the contrast between the organic or diagetic and the formal or nondiagetic in that medium. In the case of a stage play, we may forget for long periods of time that we are in a theatre facing a stage with all its contrivance. In a movie, the camera is constantly stopping and starting, creating shots that are only seconds in length. That does not necessarily destroy the illusion or deny us sustained access to the world of the film, but it does point up the disparity between the fictional world of the film and the devices used to create it.

The organic segment in a play is closely akin to Constantin Stanislavski's idea of the "beat" or "motivational unit." He, of course, developed this idea out of the actor's need to break down the progression of a role. Scenes develop as characters' motivations shift in interaction with one another. For a period of time, one motivation dominates the scene, but then it is supplanted by another one. Perhaps the motivation is thwarted and so shifts in a new direction. Or it may experience success and move on to new challenges. In other words, characters usually want something and they do things to get it. The audience is involved to the extent that it senses these motivations operating in the action. So, a **beat** is a sequence of action during which one motivation dominates. When it subsides and another motivation emerges, a new beat begins. Stanislavski also spoke of a character's "superobjective," the overarching drive or motivation of the character—that which ultimately drives the character. The shifting motivations within the beats are simply adjustments made on the road to the superobjective.

Organic segments are slightly different. Whereas the beat is based on shifting motivations, the organic segment is based on shifting tensions. Naturally, any time a motivation shifts, the tension shifts. It is also true, however, that tensions can shift for reasons other than a change in motivation. Outside forces may shift direction, new circumstance may trigger a new tension, or the atmosphere may be infused with a new tension. More often than not, these changes will feed into character motivation, but it is really the shift in tension that constitutes the end of one organic segment and the beginning of another.

One other type of temporal unit deserves mention: the **French scene.** A French scene is a sequence of action conducted among a single group of characters. As long as no one exits and no one enters, we remain within the French scene. In other words, a French scene begins and ends with an entrance or an exit. Naturally, such a segment of time is formal in the sense that an actor moving from offstage to onstage is a formal act of theatre. It is also organic inasmuch as the character portrayed by the actor is arriving here from somewhere. With that arrival, almost inevitably the tension will shift. The play is starting a new organic segment.

Shifting Tensions: Examples of Organic Segments

The important unit in dramatic structure is the organic segment. The formal segment tells us much about the overall arc of action. When a scene or an act comes to an end, we can assume that a major tension has snapped and resolved. That underlying tension will have served as a base for the variations that make up the internal, organic segments. These are the most revealing of a play's structure of action. Analyzing a play in temporal terms requires that we recognize how tensions shift and what forces operate in those shifts. In the process, of course, we must not forget that all action takes place in a context. Indeed, that context may very well deliver one or more of the forces at work.

One caveat: Isolating organic segments is not an exact science. One person might sense a shift at a point other than that experienced by a different person. Moreover, there are always occasions when a subtle change occurs and yet the alignment of tensions does not really alter. Such subtle changes create subsegments. The question is always whether the tensions truly shift. If so, we enter a new organic segment. The important point here is to discover the overall pattern of shifting tensions. That, coupled with the overall tension of the formal segment, will reveal structure clearly.

Perhaps the best way to illustrate the process is with examples from plays structured in contrasting ways. Following are sequences from three very different plays. Each sequence is long enough to contain at least three segments and part of a fourth.

The first is a scene from Shakespeare's *Othello*. The context in which this scene takes place is a room in the castle on Cyprus. Othello has married the fair Desdemona and immediately afterward been sent to Cyprus to defend the Venetian outpost against the Turks. There Iago maliciously plants poisonous seeds of jealousy in the mind of Othello, hinting that Desdemona has betrayed him and is making love with Cassio. Now that poison has begun to work, as Othello enters and encounters Iago, whom he has been seeking. A single slash indicates a subsegment break; a double slash signals an organic segment break:

OTHELLO: Ha! Ha! False to me?   1

IAGO: Why, how now, general! No more of that.

OTHELLO: Avaunt! Be gone! Thou hast set me on the rack.
   // I swear 'tis better to be much abused   2
   Than but to know a little.

IAGO: How now, my lord!

OTHELLO: What sense had I of her stol'n hours of lust?
   I saw 't not, thought it not, it harmed not me:
   I slept the next night well, was free and merry;
   I found not Cassio's kisses on her lips:
   He that is robb'd, not wanting what is stol'n,
   Let him not know 't and he's not robb'd at all.

IAGO: I am sorry to hear this.

OTHELLO: I had been happy, if the general camp,
   Pioneers and all, had tasted her sweet body,
   So I had nothing known. // O, farewell,   3
   Farewell the tranquil mind! Farewell content!
   Farewell the plumed troop and the big wars
   That make ambition virtue! O, farewell,
   Farewell the neighing steed and the shrill trump,
   The spirit-stirring drum, the ear-piercing fife,
   The royal banner and all quality,
   Pride, pomp and circumstance of glorious war!
   And, O you mortal engines, whose rude throats
   The immortal Jove's dread clamors counterfeit,
   Farewell! Othello's occupation's gone!

IAGO: Is 't possible, my lord?

OTHELLO: // Villain, be sure thou prove my love a whore;   4
   Be sure of it; give me the ocular proof;
   Or, by the worth of man's eternal soul,
   Thou hadst been better have been born a dog
   Than answer my waked wrath!

IAGO: Is 't come to this?

OTHELLO: / Make me to see 't; or at the least so prove it,
That the probation bear no hinge nor loop
To hang a doubt on; or woe upon thy life!

IAGO: My noble lord,—

OTHELLO: If thou dost slander her and torture me,
Never pray more; abandon all remorse;
On horror's head horrors accumulate;
Do deeds to make heaven weep, all earth amazed;
For nothing canst thou to damnation add
Greater than that.

IAGO: O grace! O heaven defend me!
Are you a man? Have you a soul or sense?
God be wi' you; take mine office. // O wretched fool,   5
That livest to make thine honesty a vice!
O monstrous world! Take note, take note, O world,
To be direct and honest is not safe.
I thank you for this profit, and from hence
I'll love no friend sith love breeds such offence.

OTHELLO: / Nay, stay: thou shouldst be honest.

IAGO: I should be wise; for honesty's a fool,
And loses that it works for.

OTHELLO: // By the world,   6
I think my wife be honest, and think she is not;
I think that thou art just, and I think thou art not;
I'll have some proof. Her name, that was as fresh
As Dian's visage, is now begrimed and black
As mine own face. If there be cords or knives,
Poison, or fire, or suffocating streams,
I'll not endure it. // Would I were satisfied!   7

IAGO: I see, sir, you are eaten up with passion:
I do repent me that I put it to you.
You would be satisfied?

This sequence contains six full segments and moves into a seventh. Note that they are all brief, in this instance because Othello is so conflicted that he jumps quickly and often from self-absorption to attacks on Iago. As a result, the shifts come in quick succession, and there are only two instances of a subsegment, one found in the middle of organic segment 4 and the other toward the end of segment 5. The tension shifts back and forth. In segment 1, Othello is attacking Iago, accusing him of having put him on the rack. But in segment 2, he becomes caught up in reflection. He thinks he would have been better off not knowing of Desdemona's deception, which he refers to as though he accepts her adultery as fact. In segment 3, he virtually blocks Iago out of his mind and fears the coming chaos that will torture his spirit. Suddenly, in segment 4 Othello attacks Iago, threatening him with his wrath should Iago's suggestions prove false. A subtle shift midway in this segment occurs when Othello directly orders Iago to give him "ocular proof." Iago shifts the ground in segment 5 by hinting that in this world it is not safe to be honest, implying that he has been direct and frank with Othello and deserves no punishment. Othello then shifts the ground slightly, breaking into a subsegment, with his order that Iago be honest, but this movement does not truly realign the tension. This happens soon after: Othello again becomes reflective, weighing his impulse to think Desdemona honest or Iago, for they cannot both be so. Segment 7 begins with Othello's demand that Iago satisfy him that the charges are true. In the script not reproduced here, Iago decides to oblige him with a story of hearing Cassio talk of his love for Desdemona in his sleep and then with an account of finding her handkerchief in Cassio's lodgings, a handkerchief that Iago himself has surreptitiously obtained for just this purpose. By the end of the scene, Othello is on the brink of madness.

In contrast, here is a comic scene from Molière's *Tartuffe*. It too moves forward with a series of shifts in tension, most of them ironic and incongruous, as it recounts a lovers' quarrel produced by the absurd posturing, first of the man, Valère, then of the woman, Mariane. Dorine, the maidservant, ultimately acts as referee. As background to this moment, Orgon, Mariane's father, has decided to give her in marriage to his pietistic hypocrite of a friend, Tartuffe, despite having earlier promised her to Valère. Valère has gotten wind of this development and comes to ask Mariane about it. The scene begins with his entrance:

VALÈRE: I have just heard a fine piece of news. Something I was quite
    unaware of!   **1**

MARIANE: What is it?

VALÈRE: That you are to marry Tartuffe.

MARIANE: That is certainly my father's intention.

VALÈRE: But your father . . .

MARIANE: He's changed his mind. He has just put the new proposal to
    me now.

VALÈRE: What, seriously?

MARIANE: Yes, seriously. He's determined on the match.

VALÈRE: And what is your intention?

MARIANE: I don't know.

VALÈRE: That's a fine answer! You don't know?

MARIANE: No.

VALÈRE: No?

MARIANE: What do you advise me to do?

VALÈRE: What do I advise you to do? // I advise you to take him!   **2**

MARIANE: *You* advise me to do that?

VALÈRE: Yes.

MARIANE: You really mean it?

VALÈRE: Of course. It's a splendid offer—one well worth considering.

MARIANE: / Very well, sir, I'll take your advice.

VALÈRE: I don't doubt you'll find little difficulty in doing so.

MARIANE: No more than you in offering it.

VALÈRE: I gave it to please you.

DORINE: *(Aside.)* We'll see what will come of this!

VALÈRE: // So this is how you love me! You were deceiving me
when . . .   **3**

MARIANE: Don't let us talk of that please! You told me frankly that I
should accept the husband I was offered. Well then, that's just what I
intend to do—since you give me such salutary advice.

VALÈRE: Don't make what I said your excuse! You had already made
up your mind. You're just seizing on a frivolous pretext to justify
breaking your word.

MARIANE: That's true. You put it very well.

VALÈRE: Of course! You never really loved me at all.

MARIANE: / Alas! You may think so if you like.

VALÈRE: Yes, yes. I may indeed: // but I may yet forestall your design.
I know on whom to bestow both my hand and my affections.   **4**

MARIANE: Oh! I don't doubt that in the least, and the love which your
good qualities inspire . . .

VALÈRE: Good Lord! Let's leave my good qualities out of it. They are
slight enough and your behavior is proof of it. But I know someone
who will, I hope, consent to repair my loss once she knows I am free.

MARIANE: Your loss is little enough and, no doubt, you'll easily be
consoled by the change.

VALÈRE: I shall do what I can you may be sure. // To find oneself jilted
is a blow to one's pride. One must do one's best to forget it and if one   **5**
doesn't succeed, at least one must pretend to, for to love where one's
love is scorned is an unpardonable weakness.

MARIANE: A very elevated and noble sentiment, I'm sure.

VALÈRE: Of course and one that everyone must approve. / Would you
have me languish for you indefinitely, see you throw yourself into
the arms of another and yet not bestow elsewhere the heart that you
spurn?

MARIANE: // On the contrary, that is just what I want. I only wish it
were done already.   **6**

VALÈRE: That's what you would like?

MARIANE: Yes.

> **VALÈRE:** You have insulted me sufficiently. You shall have your wish . . . \ *(Makes a move to go)* and immediately!
>
> **MARIANE:** Very well.

This exchange has a sort of seesaw effect, and it produces comic shifts of tension that occasion new organic segments. In the first segment, Valère simply wants to find out if it is true that Orgon has changed his mind, reneged on his promise, and has now selected Tartuffe to be Mariane's husband. The ground shifts when she states that she does not know what she intends to do about it. He is astounded. To put her to the test, he advises her to take the alternate husband. This takes us into the second segment, when Mariane gets her back up that Valère can so freely give such advice. Segment 3 has him accusing her of never loving him, countered by her claims that he must have been looking for an excuse to call off their marriage. In the next segment, he threatens her with the news that there is another woman who will take him as soon as she knows he is free. Valère becomes introspective in the fifth segment, telling himself to be strong. Mariane's announcement that she wishes Valère were already betrothed to that other woman begins still another segment, the sixth, and now they are set to spurn and walk out on each other, which is when Dorine, who has been quiet all this time, finally intervenes and pulls the two of them back together. The slight shifts marked with a single slash in the course of the scene are not strong enough to generate a completely new organic segment. The tenser and more comical the scene becomes, the more these two feel compelled to posture and ruin any chance of reconciliation.

The last example is from a modern play, *Day of Absence*, by Douglas Turner Ward. The excerpt comes from the very beginning of the play, which lays down the fundamental conditions that help propel the action. These conditions are of two kinds: fictional and theatrical. Regarding the fictional conditions, we quickly learn that the play is set in a sleepy, bucolic southern town. It is early morning and the town is just rousing for the day ahead. We know that Luke and Clem seem to start every morning outside their adjacent shops. The theatrical conditions consist of appeals to our imagination to create the street and storefronts out of the simple suggestion of the store signs and the platforms on which the two men sit. Another such appeal comes as the two men wave to imaginary passersby. After a brief moment, we recognize still another theatrical condition: Clem and Luke are played by black actors in white face. The same will hold true of every character in the play except two: a white television anchorman and Rastus, played by a black actor "in his native hue." Ward calls the play "a reverse minstrel show," and indeed many playgoers will be readily reminded of that old theatrical tradition as Clem and Luke emerge as ironic versions of Mr. Bones and Tambo. In a sense, the first organic segment of the play occurs as we notice these suggestions and even before the dialogue begins. For the sake of convenience, the first segment begins with actual action:

> **CLEM:** *(Sitting under a sign suspended by invisible wires and bold-printed with the lettering: "STORE.")* 'Morning, Luke. . . .   1
>
> **LUKE:** *(Sitting a few paces away under an identical sign.)* 'Morning, Clem . . .

CLEM: Go'n' be a hot day.

LUKE: Looks that way. . . .

CLEM: Might rain though. . . .

LUKE: Might.

CLEM: Hope it does . . .

LUKE: Me, too . . .

CLEM: Farmers could use a little wet spell for a change. . . . How's the Missis?

LUKE: Same.

CLEM: 'N' the kids?

LUKE: Them too. . . . How's yourns?

CLEM: Fine, thank you. . . . /

(They both lapse into drowsy silence waving lethargically from time to time at imaginary passersby.)

CLEM: Hi, Joe.

LUKE: Joe. . . .

CLEM: . . . How'd it go yesterday, Luke?

LUKE: Fair.

CLEM: Same wit' me. . . . Business don't seem to git no better or no worse. Guess we in a rut, Luke, don't it 'pear that way to you? . . . Morning, ma'am.

LUKE: Morning. . . .

CLEM: Tried display, sales, advertisement, stamps—everything, yet merchandising stumbles 'round in the same old groove. . . . But— that's better than plunging downwards, I reckon.

LUKE: Guess it is.

CLEM: Morning, Bret. How's the family? . . . That's good.

LUKE: Bret . . .

CLEM: Morning, Sue.

LUKE: How do, Sue. /

CLEM: *(Staring after her.)* . . . Fine hunk of woman.

LUKE: Sure is.

CLEM: Wonder if it's any good?

LUKE: Bet it is.

CLEM: Sure like to find out!

LUKE: So would I.

CLEM: You ever try?

LUKE: Never did. . . .

CLEM: Morning, Gus. . . .

LUKE: 'Howdy, Gus.

CLEM: Fine, thank you.

(They lapse into silence again. // CLEM rouses himself slowly, begins to look around quizzically.)   2

CLEM: Luke . . . ?

LUKE: Huh?

CLEM: Do you . . . er, er . . . feel anything—funny . . . ?

LUKE: Like what?

CLEM: Like . . . er . . . something—strange?

LUKE: I dunno . . . haven't thought about it.

CLEM: I mean . . . like something's wrong—outta place, unusual?

LUKE: I don't know. . . . What you got in mind?

CLEM: Nothing . . . just that . . . just that . . . like somp'ums outa kilter. I got a funny feeling somp'ums not up to snuff. Can't figger out what it is. . . .

LUKE: Maybe it's in your haid?

CLEM: No, not like that. . . . Like somp'ums happened . . . or happening— gone haywire, loony.

LUKE: Well, don't worry about it, it'll pass.

CLEM: Guess you right. *(Attempts return to somnolence but doesn't succeed.)* . . . I'm sorry, Luke, but you sure you don't feel nothing peculiar . . . ?

LUKE: / *(Slightly irked.)* Toss it out of your mind, Clem. We got a long day ahead of us. If something's wrong, you'll know 'bout it in due time. No use worrying about it 'til it comes and if it's coming, it will. Now, relax!

\ CLEM: All right, you right. . . . Hi, Margie. . . .

LUKE: Marge.

CLEM: *(Unable to control himself.)* Luke, I don't give a damn what you say. Somp'ums topsy-turvy, I just know it!

LUKE: *(Increasingly irritated.)* Now look here, Clem—it's a bright day, it looks like it's go'n' git hotter. You say the wife and kids are fine and the business is no better or no worse? Well, what else could be wrong? . . . if somp'ums go'n' happen, it's go'n' happen anyway and there ain't a damn fool thing you kin do to stop it! So you ain't helping me, yourself or nobody else by thinking 'bout it. It's not go'n' be no better or no worse when it gits here. It'll come to you when it gits ready to come and it's go'n' be the same whether you worry about it or not. So stop letting it upset you!

(Luke settles back in his chair. Clem does likewise. Luke shuts his eyes. After a few moments, they reopen. He forces them shut again. // They reopen in greater curiosity. Finally, he rises slowly to an upright position in the chair, looks around frowningly. Turns slowly to Clem.)   3

LUKE: . . . Clem? . . . You know something? . . . Somp'um is peculiar. . . .

CLEM: *(Vindicated.)* I knew it, Luke! I just knew it! Ever since we been sitting here, I been having that feeling!

Blackout

This completes a full formal segment from lights up to blackout. Momentarily, lights will come back up on a couple lying under a blanket on a platform placed under another sign with the lettering "HOME." We gain the impression that we will be moving around town as it is affected by this mysterious situation that Clem and Luke are the first to notice.

Within this excerpted formal segment are three organic segments: The first establishes the somnolent lethargy normal to the town; Clem starts the second with his sudden awareness that something is out of kilter, peculiar, not up to snuff; and Luke ushers in the third as he too senses something wrong. There are subtle shifts within these segments, as when the imaginary passersby appear or when Clem is turned on by the sight of Sue, but they do not entirely realign the tensions.

The scene, the entire formal segment, portrays the disruption of the normal state of affairs in this town. The disruption is obvious even though the origin remains mysterious. The disruption becomes a little clearer in the second scene when John and Mary are awakened by their crying baby and the maid is not there to tend to it. By the third scene, in the telephone office, the disruption becomes fully clear: Every single black person has disappeared. Clem and Luke had sensed their absence, but having grown used to looking right through such people, they cannot put their finger on what is so peculiar this morning. Only when the maid is not there to change the diaper, nor the janitor to empty the trash, nor the chauffeur to polish the mayor's limousine do the white townspeople realize the disaster that is upon them. The town in fact is declared a disaster area. High-powered hoses fail to flush out any black people from the town jail. Neighboring towns refuse to loan any of their blacks. The mayor goes on national television to appeal to the lost blacks, wherever they are, to come home. The action rises to a fever pitch of anxiety and panic. The final scene takes up with Clem and Luke out on their chairs the next morning, but this time they become aware of an approaching figure:

LUKE: *(gazing in silent fascination at the approaching figure)* . . . Clem . . . ? Do see you what I see, or am I dreaming . . . ?

CLEM: It's a . . . Nigra, ain't it, Luke . . . ?

LUKE: Sure looks like one, Clem—but we better make sure—eyes could be playing tricks on us. . . . Does he still look like one to you, Clem?

CLEM: He still does, Luke—but I'm scared to believe—

LUKE: . . . Why . . . ? It looks like Rastus, Clem!

CLEM: Sure does, Luke . . . But we better not jump to no hasty conclusion. . . .

LUKE: *(in timid softness.)* That you, Rastus . . . ?

RASTUS: *(Steppin Fetchit, Willie Best, Nicodemus and B. McQueen all the rest rolled into one.)* Why . . . Howdy . . . Mr. Luke . . . Mr. Clem.

CLEM: It is him, Luke! It is him!

LUKE: Rastus?

RASTUS: Yeas . . . sah?

LUKE: Where was you yesterday?

RASTUS: *(very, very puzzled.)* Yes . . . ter . . . day? . . . Yester . . . day . . . ? Why . . . right . . . Here . . . Mr. Luke. . . .

LUKE: No you warn't, Rastus, don't lie to me! Where was you yestiddy?

RASTUS: Why . . . I'm sure I was . . . Mr. Luke. . . . Remember . . . I made . . . that . . . Delivery for you . . .

LUKE: That was MONDAY, Rastus, yestiddy was TUESDAY.

RASTUS: Tues . . . day . . . ? You don't say. . . . Well . . . well . . . well . . .

LUKE: Where was you 'n' all the other Nigras yesterday, Rastus?

RASTUS: I . . . thought . . . yestiddy . . . was . . . Monday, Mr. Luke—I coulda swore it . . . ! . . . See how . . . things . . . kin git all mixed up? . . . I coulda swore it . . .

LUKE: TODAY is WEDNESDAY, Rastus. Where was you TUESDAY?

RASTUS: Tuesday . . . huh? That's sump'um. . . . I . . . don't . . . remember . . . missing . . . day . . . Mr. Luke . . . but I guess you right . . .

LUKE: Then where was you!!!???

RASTUS: Don't rightly know, Mr. Luke. I didn't know I had skipped a day. But that jist goes to show you how time kin fly, don't it, Mr.Luke . . . Uuh, uuh, uuh . . . *(He starts shuffling off, scratching head, a flicker of a smile playing across his lips.* **Clem** *and* **Luke** *gaze dumbfoundedly as he disappears.)*

LUKE: *(eyes sweeping around in all directions.)* Well. . . . There's the others, Clem. . . . Back jist like they useta be. . . . Everything's same as always . . .

CLEM: ??? . . . Is it. . . . Luke . . . !

(Slow fade. Curtain.)

This is the end of the play, with a formal segment composed of one organic segment. The mystery of the day of absence is still there, but it appears that Rastus ("a flicker of a smile playing across his lips") knows something the white folks don't know, and Clem at least finds that unsettling.

Phases of Dramatic Action

The two excerpts from *Day of Absence* serve another purpose here. While they illus-trate the behavior of organic segments and formal segments, they also give us an indication of the arc of action that typically completes a play. As stated earlier, a play begins in some state of equipoise. Suddenly an incident disturbs that balance and produces a will to redress the situation, to put it somehow back to rights. This will, most often embodied in the protagonist, moves the play forward against all sorts of odds until it arrives at a point of no return, when the issue must be settled. Once the will has its way or is fully stymied, tension snaps and the world falls into some new state of equipoise. *Day of Absence* is a little peculiar in that it is a com-munity play, and the townspeople as a whole embody the will, only to be thwarted: They may have their "Nigras" back, but not on the same terms as before. Otherwise the play follows this arc closely.

This description of the arc of action lends itself to analysis of a series of phases that make up the movement of the action. We have often heard them referred to as rising action and falling action, or as exposition, inciting incident, complications, crisis, climax, and resolution. These are all perfectly apt terms. In them we can recognize the spirit of an arc of action. Nevertheless, they present a subtle difficulty. They tend to treat the play as a self-contained world consisting merely of an internal structure. Although it is true that plays depend on struc-ture, this structure builds not only on story but also on the theatrical context and most of all on the presence of an audience. In fact, some plays depend much more on these last two factors and barely have a retellable story. What follows is an adaptation of these traditional phases of dramatic action, taking into account not only plot or story but also those factors that derive from context and audience involvement.

We might lay these phases out in the following manner:

1. The establishment of context, in both theatrical and fictional terms:
   a. Theatrical conventions
   b. Probability
   c. Exposition
2. Inciting incident: the disturbing event
3. Emergence of the driving will, occurring usually immediately on the heels of the inciting incident
4. Resistance: obstacles that the will strives to overcome:
   a. Contrary wills
   b. Circumstance
   c. Discoveries
   d. Reversals
5. Crisis, the moment of decision when the central issue must be faced
6. Climax, the decision, which snaps the tension that has caught up the audi-ence, following hard on the heels of the crisis
7. Dénouement, the unraveling of tension and the reestablishment of equipoise

To these we might add the initial impression that the very first moment creates in the audience and the final impression the play leaves the audience as the stage lights fade and the world of the play evaporates.

Although the phases as listed may not seem all that different from the traditional set of terms, examining them with an eye to how they operate on a stage and in confrontation with an audience can make a significant difference in our analysis. No play really speaks its own mind fully. They all meet their audiences at least part way. In a good play, the audience is actively involved in exercising imagination, histrionic sensibility, judgment, and reflection. Rarely do audience members see things exactly as the characters do. Moreover, they rarely accept anything at face value. There is always some degree of ironic interplay between the play's action and the audience's perception of it. Nevertheless, the audience is designed into the script. When we read a script, we can sense the anticipated contribution of the audience. It is part of the structure—so much so that we can enjoy reading a script in the same spirit that we would watch the play with an audience, albeit much less intensely.

The Establishment of Context

Three factors contribute to the context in which a play's action develops: conventions, probability, and exposition. The first has to do with the theatrical context, the manner in which the play invites the audience's participation. The last has to do with the internal world the characters occupy. Meanwhile, probability is the link between the first and last. Every one of these factors has to do with creating a rapport with the audience.

Convention consists of giving the audience an understanding of how it is to engage its collective imagination with the actual events performed on stage. Plays are not real life and for the most part they do not pretend to be. The characters are not literally there before our eyes. The complete world they live in cannot be fully represented or duplicated. We have to agree to accept the things the actors do and the stage space they occupy as being something quite different, but we are not going to agree unless we know the terms of the agreement. That is convention. It is a sort of contract between play and audience. If we cannot accept the contract, the play will never engage us. Some people, for example, find it hard to engage with Greek tragedy simply because they are unaccustomed to the convention of the chorus, this group of people who are half in the play as characters, occasionally interjecting themselves in chants and dance movements, and half outside the play watching it with us. Opera functions on the convention that people will converse in recitatives and express emotion in arias. European plays of the seventeenth and eighteenth centuries allow characters to slide in and out of their imagined domains with "asides" to the audience, remarks that we hear but that the other characters cannot hear. Elizabethan playwrights, including Shakespeare, from time to time have an actor stand alone on stage talking, and we by convention accept that the actor is a character thinking. Even in the case of a realistic play, in which actors appear to talk and move about just as people do in real life, we accept the convention that these characters are moving about in a room with four walls, the fourth one transparent to our gaze: The actors—but not the characters—know they are being watched.

A play is a form of communication. As such, it has to spell out its "language" clearly enough for the audience to see through the stage and its activity into the virtual world of the characters. Although conventions are agreed on, convention is not merely a matter of tapping traditional understandings about how the stage operates. It includes the subtleties of how each individual play opens itself to its audience—and each play does so in a slightly unique way. This window into the play might be provocative, as in the reverse minstrel show implied in *Day of Absence*. It might be an overt speech to the audience that invites us into a character's memory, as in the case of Tennessee Williams's *Glass Menagerie*. Or it might consist of a narrator, a storyteller, who conjures up the actors to illustrate his tale, as in Bertolt Brecht's *Caucasian Chalk Circle*. We will accept any of these as long as the terms are clear enough, sooner or later.

Probability was described in Chapter 2 as "internal probability" or "Aristotelian probability." This too has to be established early in a play. What sort of world is the one we are encountering? Audiences want to know what kinds of things happen in this fictional world of the play. Many things contribute to probability, and it is important because the audience must find the play believable, not by what is likely to happen in the real world but by what might well happen given the terms laid down for the play's world. These terms emerge in the opening moments of most plays. They may even begin with the title of the play. If we hear the title *The Bald Soprano*, a short play by Eugène Ionesco, we know that we are likely to enter into a realm of unreality. When the curtain opens on that play, Mr. Smith appears seated behind his newspaper with Mrs. Smith nearby darning socks as the grandfather clock chimes seventeen times. Now it is clear that a special probability is at work.

More than general believability feeds into the sense of probability. The alignment of tensions, often evident in the first few moments, also contributes. We come to expect certain sorts of things to happen by our sensitivity to those tensions. References might be made to things or people "out there" in the next room or on the street. We might hear how things once were, perhaps a year ago. One part of the stage might stand in contrast to another. Character groupings might suggest tensions. Any of these things may be apparent even before the disturbance of the inciting incident. In the case of Tom Stoppard's *The Real Inspector Hound*, we are confronted with an empty drawing room, on the other side of which is a fake, painted audience in whose midst we discern two critics. It is they who start the play: "Has it started yet?" says one. "I believe it's a pause," says the other, to which the first retorts, "Good God, you can't start with a pause." The tension between the play-within-the-play and the critics watching it becomes the very basis for the dramatic action. Anton Chekhov's *The Three Sisters* starts with the three sisters, each isolated and preoccupied, the silence between them then broken by Olga's line, "Father died a year ago." This play is ultimately about isolation in time, the sisters cut off from a better time before father died and when they lived in Moscow. That tension is already established with the first impression and the first line.

Exposition is the third of the three factors that contribute to the establishment of context. The term refers to the laying out of information about the characters, their identities, their past, and their present situation. We don't learn everything about them at the very beginning of a play. We will learn new things all the way through the play, often to the very end. Exposition, at least in good plays, occurs throughout the play; it is not a distinct phase at the outset. Nevertheless, we need to know enough to feel oriented and to arouse our curiosity. We are, after all, just meeting new people. One way or another, when we encounter characters in the midst of living their lives, a tension arises just by our "arrival." Harold Pinter was fascinated by the experience we have all had of walking into a room already occupied by persons we don't quite know engaged in an activity we know nothing about. In fact, he based many of his early plays on this concept, including, appropriately enough, *The Room.* This is the spirit of the theatrical encounter: Who are these people? What are they up to? How did things come to this pass?

Although not literally exposition, in the sense of information about the characters, tone also enters into our initial encounter with a play. We want not only to know about the characters but also to know what to make of them. Are they awesome, powerful, inspiring? Perhaps they are gentle, everyday souls, or outrageous stereotypes, or buffoons, or dark and evil schemers. The early portion of the play gives a strong hint of the playwright's tone, the attitude we come to share with the author if the play is at all successful. As mentioned before, characterization applies not only to the characters that make up the cast but also to the audience.

Inciting Incident and Emergence of the Driving Force

Despite all the matters that must be settled in the initial phase of a play, the establishment of context is relatively brief. Good plays start fast. Something happens and the world is thrown out of joint. The event is powerful enough to elicit a will to redress the imbalance, to put the world back to rights. It incites action. As in life, it is usually too late to put the world back the way it was. Nevertheless, the new state of affairs is unacceptable; something must be done. This is called the **inciting incident** because it incites the **emergence of the driving force.** Oedipus learns that the plague will be lifted only when the murderer of the previous king is expelled from Thebes (inciting incident); he curses the murderer and sets out to find him (emergence of the driving force). Hamlet meets the ghost of his father, who tells him that his Uncle Claudius killed him, and the ghost charges Hamlet with avenging him (inciting incident); Hamlet sets about the task, first trying to ascertain the truth of what the ghost has said (emergence of driving force.)

These are clear cases of the juncture between inciting incident and emergence of driving force. Sometimes the connection is more subtle, perhaps because the driving force is not embodied in a single character. In the case of *Tartuffe,* for example, Orgon has taken in the lascivious, hypocritical, self-righteous Tartuffe and promised him his daughter in marriage (inciting incident); the entire household (especially the maid Dorine, the brother-in-law Cléante, and the wife Elmire) bands together to drive Tartuffe from the house. It takes a greater force than they can muster, and ultimately it is the offstage king who manages finally to evict the scoundrel. Or perhaps the inciting incident produces a mysterious state of affairs that has to be understood if it is to be dealt with. In Tom Stoppard's *Rosencrantz and Guildenstern Are Dead,* the title characters become aware that they are operating in uncharted waters when the king of Denmark summons them to the court. They simply don't know what it is all about; all they feel sure of is that the situation poses some threat to their well-being. This is the inciting incident provoked by flipping coins that refuse to come up anything but heads. The driving force is their effort to understand the situation and gain control of it. Generally, action needs an agent and most often that agent must be a character with whom we identify on some level. There are, of course, exceptions. In Anton Chekhov's *The Three Sisters,* the sisters express a fervent and yet vague wish to return to Moscow, where they expect their lives to somehow be as they once were. That, strangely enough, is the inciting incident, followed almost at once by the news of the arrival in town of Colonel Vershinin and by other distractions that accumulate to the point that we sense the driving force to be the passage of time and life itself. The sisters cannot quite observe that passage, and certainly cannot control it, and the result is that they not only do not go to Moscow, but they also are driven out of their house into lives they never planned or expected.

The point should now be apparent that the inciting incident and the emergence of the driving force together set up the action of the play. They lay down the central tension, the will to do something and the resistance that works against this will. They set up our anticipation, the overarching action of the play, and some kind of coherence whereby ultimately we can judge the play to be legitimately over when the curtain falls. When this is not the case, the play becomes a string of activities rather than an overarching action. It could be over at any time or could continue endlessly. The appeal of drama, whether serious or comic, lies in the spectacle of striving. If the characters encounter no difficulty about accomplishing a goal, the play might as well be over and done with at once. To satisfy this need, the bulk of a play's action consists of the will encountering resistance, frequently in multiple forms

Resistance

This phase of a play's action constitutes the fullest measure of its development. It is the so-called rising action during which the driving force must deal with adversity, all the way up to its most crucial confrontation. Resistance is the meat of the play. Resistance will arise from a multitude of sources: from other characters whose wishes run counter to the driving force, from obstacles that grow out of the inherent circumstance, from unexpected conditions, from unanticipated results of an action, and so forth. Oedipus, for example, encounters resistance in such factors as the apparent duplicity of Teiresias and Creon, from Jocasta's efforts to divert him from his purpose, from the reluctance of the shepherd to say what he knows, and from Oedipus's own dawning recognition that he is himself the murderer he seeks. Similarly, Hamlet finds resistance in his doubts about the legitimacy of the ghost, in the suspicions that Claudius and Polonius harbor of him, in his concern for and disappointment in Gertrude, in his love for Ophelia, in his mistaken murder of Polonius, in being sent off to England, and in the enmity he inspires in Laertes. In both of these cases, a thread binds together all the opposing forces. For Oedipus it is the decreed fate that he ultimately cannot avoid, and for Hamlet it is the corrupt, manipulative, and threatening world of the court of Denmark.

In very general terms, resistance comes in two forms: as an antagonistic force or as a circumstance. Both are rendered dramatically through a process of discovery and reversal. Nobody, neither the characters nor the audience, ever knows quite everything. In good plays, a careful pattern of irony develops about who knows what when. The forward movement of a play derives partly from curiosity. One character does not know something that another does know, and it would make all the difference for that first character to find it out. Meanwhile, the audience may know things that a character needs to know, and we wait for the moment when the character discovers it. For this reason, discovery can provide quick and compelling shifts in the dramatic action. Reversals, moments when an action has an unexpected result, are themselves a form of discovery, and they also produce new turns in the plot. At the outset, we in the audience know next to nothing, whereas the characters, who have supposedly been living their lives all along, are well aware of their situations. It is like stumbling into a room unannounced and trying to get on the wavelength of what is happening. Gradually we catch on. After a while, we may even surpass some of the characters in knowledge, or we may perceive things in a distinctly different way. The chorus in *Oedipus* rejoices at the news of the death of the king of Corinth, but we know better. Audience members acquainted with *Hamlet* know what will happen to Rosencrantz and Guildenstern in Tom Stoppard's play, and others can take a hint from the title, *Rosencrantz and Guildenstern Are Dead.* For the drama, there is special meaning in the old adage, "Life is what happens when you are making other plans."

This dissonance is actually not just a matter of disparity of knowledge between characters and audience. It may also be a disparity in perception or even wisdom. We see Blanche DuBois with very different eyes than does Stanley—or even Stella. We can see the disaster that the characters in *The Cherry Orchard* are creating for themselves while they remain blind to it. We see the capitulation of Brecht's Galileo in a very different light than he does himself. And, although we share the confusion of perception that the six characters exhibit in Pirandello's play, we can sense the crumbling of their play-within-the-play long before they or the Director come to terms with it—and in fact they never do.

We can usually look back on the entire action of a play, especially through the resistance phase, and sort out its major landmarks. These are moments when things change drastically and take new direction. They are also moments that diminish the options for the driving force. Eventually will come a time, a point of no return, when the driving force confronts the root source of all the resistance. This takes us to the next phase: the crisis and climax of the action.

Crisis and Climax

These two terms are often confused with each other. **Crisis** is the moment of decision when the central issue must be faced. **Climax** is the decision itself. Once made, the tension that has played into the rising action of the play snaps. The crisis occurs when the driving force encounters the source of all resistance—the counterforce. In a blatant melodrama, the crisis is the gun duel at high noon in the center of town. Such plays work so hard to affect their audiences that their bones show. Nevertheless, even subtle plays bring us to a point of built-up tension that promises finally to fulfill our anticipation. We might think of this as satisfying the play's **major dramatic question.** Blatant mystery dramas are called "whodunits," which is essentially a major dramatic question. We might think of *Oedipus Rex* as a whodunit, except that we more or less know who did it, and we are more consumed by the curiosity of what he will do when he finds out that he himself is the murderer he is seeking. The major dramatic question for *Hamlet* is "Will Hamlet succeed in avenging his father's death?" Both of these are great plays, and distilling the major dramatic question for each does not diminish them. It simply exposes their frameworks.

In the middle of the nineteenth century, when the "well-made play" was enormously popular, the framework was all important. The formula for the well-made play was so tight that playwrights such as Eugène Scribe and Victorien Sardou were able to churn out scripts by the score using a formula based on keeping audience members on the edge of their seats by astonishing reversals, stunning discoveries, cliff-hanger act endings, and highly tense crises. Writing about these plays, critic Francisque Sarcey coined the term "obligatory scene," the scene in the play that presents the culmination of all the tension. It is obligatory simply because it satisfies the anticipation that built up from the beginning of the play. The audience in effect demands to see the ultimate confrontation and will become testy and annoyed if denied it. Essentially, the obligatory scene begins with the crisis moment. We know now that the characters must face the fundamental issue. By the end of the scene, we feel assured that the driving force will either triumph or go down in defeat. That decisive moment is the climax of the play, snapping the tension once and for all.

It could be argued that all this applies only to formulaic, linear, cause-to-effect dramatic structures. There are alternatives, structures based on juxtaposition or montage, others based on a kind of circularity. These alternatives may not push the crisis and climax into strong relief, but they do nevertheless feature some arc of action that rounds out with the release of tension. The release may not be abrupt and powerful. We might not even notice it when it occurs, but afterward we can look back and locate the moment when the tension is no longer there. Chekhov's *The Cherry Orchard,* for example, is not a formulaic play, so much of it transpiring below the surface. It has a climax moment that is quiet and muted but nevertheless there. The major dramatic question is "Will the Ranevsky family manage to save their estate and way of life?" We feel certain from early in the play that they will not. And yet we keep hoping they will seize the moment and finally do something that will make the difference. By the fourth and last act, they have lost the estate at auction to their friend, Yermolay Alexeyevich Lopahin. Because he is their friend and apparently in love with the daughter, Varya, who also loves him, one last-ditch effort could keep the estate in the family: arranging for Lopahin and Varya to marry. He agrees to propose. She is sent to him and they are alone, each knowing that this is the time for action. This is the crisis that opens the obligatory scene. Instead of coming to Lopahin, Varya pretends to be searching for something:

> VARYA: *(Looking over the luggage in a leisurely fashion.)* Strange. I can't find it . . .
>
> LOPAHIN: What are you looking for?
>
> VARYA: Packed it myself and I don't remember . . . *(Pause.)*
>
> LOPAHIN: Where are you going now, Varya?
>
> VARYA: I? To the Ragulins. I've arranged to take charge there—as a house-keeper, if you like.
>
> LOPAHIN: At Yashnevo? About fifty miles from here. *(Pause.)* Well, life in this house is ended!
>
> VARYA: *(Examining the luggage.)* Where is it? Perhaps I put it in the chest. Yes, life in this house is ended. . . . There will be no more of it.
>
> LOPAHIN: And I'm just off to Kharkov—by this next train. I've a lot to do there. I'm leaving Yepihodov here. . . . I've hired him.
>
> VARYA: Oh!
>
> LOPAHIN: Last year at this time it was snowing, if you remember, but now it's sunny and there's no wind. It's cold, though . . . it must be three below.
>
> VARYA: I didn't look. *(Pause.)* And besides, our thermometer's broken.
>
> VOICE OFF: Yermolay Alexeyevich!
>
> LOPAHIN: *(As if he had been waiting for the call.)* Coming! This minute! *(He exits quickly. Varya sits on the floor and sobs quietly, her head on a bundle of clothes.)*

The climax occurs when Lopahin leaves the room without proposing, which snaps the tension. There is no further hope. The situation is settled. Indeed, this is a muted climax that might pass us by without our noticing it as such, but clearly it leaves us nothing more to anticipate. The tension is gone.

This is not the end of the play. The climax may snap the essential tension, but it does not finish all action. There is still some turbulence in the waters that must subside in order for them to flow out. In other words, the climax decides the issue and indicates the direction the resolution must take.

Dénouement

Dénouement means "unraveling" in French. It is an apt metaphor for what happens in the last phase of a play. At the outset of the action, an inciting incident causes a driving force to emerge, and as it encounters resistance the tension rises until the climactic moment of decision. Then all the tautness of the tension unravels and the world relaxes in some new state of equipoise. That is the dénouement or resolution. This phase is longer or shorter depending on how complex the issues have been. In tragedy the resolution is often somewhat longer, not only because the issues are more complex but also because when the resistance washes over the driving force, more time is required for balance to reestablish itself. Outright comedy tends to finish up quickly, usually with a joyous celebration between characters who only a short time before had been vying with one another. Comic characters are resilient and land on their feet much more readily than their tragic counterparts.

Not all plays end by wrapping everything up neatly at the final curtain. In fact, the neater the ending is, the less likely it is that the play really engaged us, for its contrivance will have blunted its outward implications for us in our world. Bertolt Brecht in his best plays placed the climax just moments before the end because he sought to leave us reeling and thinking, not because the plays are comic but because they are rich in implications about the world we live in.

Most playwrights take pains to create a vivid last image. The final impression a play leaves with its audience can make a pithy statement about all that has gone before. When we think of some of the most moving or powerful plays, we often automatically think of the last image, the play's parting shot, as it were. Henrik Ibsen's *Ghosts* ends with a searing image of Oswald going into a seizure from his illness and calling for his mother to give him the sun. The ending is ambiguous about whether she will administer the morphine that may relieve his suffering but also possibly end his life. This final impression has a close affinity with the tension that informed all the action of the play, the tension between what we feel naturally we must do and what society dictates we must do. Luigi Pirandello delivers several blows in the very last moments of *Six Characters in Search of an Author:* the sudden death of the two children in the semidarkness; the director's call for lights that results in a blinding white light; the dismissal of the actors and the plunging of the entire theatre into pitch blackness; the weird tableau of the gigantic shadows of four of the characters projected on the background scrim; and the breaking of the Stepdaughter, who runs laughing from the stage. These last images are pertinent, for this is a play about the curious ways in which we perceive reality. Still another provocative last image is found at the end of Maria Irene Fornes's *The Conduct of Life*, a play about abuse and torture. Letitia shoots her husband Orlando after suffering much abuse, turns to Nena, his child sex slave, hands the gun to her, and says, "Please." What Letitia means we can't be sure, for the play ends at that moment. She may be asking Nena to shoot her, or she may be offering her the gun in case Nena should need it against some future abuser, or she may be requesting that the gun be hidden away, or she may be asking Nena to take the blame for the murder. All of these possibilities play on our mind and remind us of the spectacle of abuse we have witnessed throughout the play. These are just three examples of how the dénouement does not necessarily simply wrap up the action of the play; it may well leave us with a challenging vision that keeps reverberating long after the show is over.

These then are the typical phases of dramatic action: establishment of context, inciting incident, emergence of the driving force, resistance, crisis, climax, and dénouement. They give a play coherence, a system of relative values, by which the audience knows what has import and what does not. They establish the ebb and flow of forces and counterforces. They provide a rhythm. They also create an arc of action that rounds out and completes the play. They are, however, only signposts in the play's progression. As we pass each of the signposts, we need to assess the nature of our involvement as audience members. In examining that relationship between the phases and our engagement, we can discover much about the play, how it operates, and even how it "means." More will be said about meaning in the next chapter.

CHAPTER

5

Form and Style in the Drama

Drama is a form of communication. It is also an experience. We in the audience undergo sensations created by the stage spectacle and the performers. We even have the sense of witnessing characters living their lives. Yet we do not confuse the play with everyday actuality. As mentioned in previous chapters, a play deliberately separates itself from reality in order to reflect on it. It cannot do so if it does not have some distance on life. It also cannot do so unless the audience can recognize and accept the terms on which the play operates. Although previous chapters have touched on this concept in connection with the principles of Aristotelian probability and theatrical convention, form and style are even more basic to this process of communicating with the audience. If we think of drama as a language, then form and style are its syntax. Form tells us what materials the play uses and how it uses them. It also tells us the attitude we are to take toward the characters and their experience. Style gives us the perspective on reality we are to take from the play. No play is absolutely unique. The closer a play comes to being truly unique, the less likely it is that audiences will know how to relate to it. Form and style are the means by which we comprehend a play.

This in turn means there is an ample measure of tradition associated with these two concepts. Avant-garde dramatists are keen on discovering new forms, but even when they seem to succeed (or perhaps especially when they succeed) there remains enough of tradition in the new form to allow for audience engagement. At any rate, it is perhaps this factor that grants a certain academic stuffiness to formal and stylistic terminology. Shakespeare pokes fun at this tendency through the speech he gives Polonius on the arrival of the players at Elsinore. He describes the players to Hamlet as being: "The best actors in the world, either for tragedy, comedy, history, pastoral, pastoral-comical, historical-pastoral, tragical-pastoral, tragical-comical-historical-pastoral, scene indivisible, or poem unlimited." Still, the ideas of form and style are inescapable. All plays must by definition take on form and conduct their action in accordance with a style. Consciously or not, every playwright must make decisions on these matters. Sometimes the playwright makes decisions with no great deliberation while addressing more immediate matters. At other times, the playwright makes calculated choices in response to problems encountered in writing. Brecht was keenly aware of his ideas of epic theatre while he wrote. Friedrich Dürrenmatt often commented on the necessity for "grotesque comedy" as he wrote such plays as *The Visit* and *The Physicists*. Arthur Miller similarly spoke of "tragedy and the common man" in connection with *Death of a Salesman*. Other playwrights make no issue of their form and style, but they are no less involved in them. The point is that all playwrights make decisions about form and style.

Seen in this way, the terms are no longer quite so abstract. They involve a very natural set of conditions. Although it is perfectly natural that a play reflects a playwright's attitude and point of view, there is a sort of two-way pull involved. Paradoxically, form and style are simultaneously private and personal and yet public and traditional. On the one hand, the playwright shapes material in accordance with his or her personal relationship to it. On the other, a play is intended always for a public audience that brings expectations—hence traditions—out of previous theatre experience. Again, no audience could relate to an absolutely unique play, even if someone could write one. Meanwhile, a play that simply fulfilled audience expectations would be tame, dull, and trite.

The Difference between Form and Style

It is difficult to draw a clear distinction between form and style because they tend to blur into each another. One way to distinguish them is to see form as a product of attitude and style as a product of point of view. This is very generally true, and if the two tend to blur, it is because attitude is heavily influenced by point of view and vice versa.

Style is a characteristic mode of expression. An artist must handle the materials of the chosen medium, but how he or she handles them is entirely up to the artist. Ultimately, it will depend on how the playwright views the world. What he or she considers important and intriguing, and why, leads him or her to slant the material one way or another, give emphasis here rather than there, and render language and action in a certain manner. Much of this is second nature, just as Harold Pinter's "weasel under the coffee table" was produced by his second nature. This is so much the case that the work of a well-known playwright is almost always immediately recognizable after only a few lines of dialogue. The material is always rooted in what the playwright values and in the perspective he or she takes on human experience. In short, style has to do with the relationship between the play and reality.

Form has to do with the play's relationship to its audience. The formal elements alert the audience as to how to relate to the play. To the extent that a play is a form of communication, it needs a reasonably recognizable form. Without it the audience cannot share the experience. How a play isolates itself in time and space helps establish audience expectations. Moreover, the suggestions of a tone or attitude early in the play signal to the audience how they are to view the experience ahead. Time and space are a matter of structural form: use of the stage, formal breaks in the action, and use of material such as dialogue, music, song, or dance. Tonal form includes tragedy, comedy, tragicomedy, melodrama, farce, and so forth.

In the traditional terminology associated with each of these concepts, form is described by such categories as comedy and tragedy; one act and full length; opera, musical comedy, dance drama, historical drama, and so forth. Style takes on the guise of various "isms": romanticism, realism, naturalism, symbolism, expressionism, and absurdism are all styles. Each handles the materials of the stage in characteristic ways determined by a vision of reality. Any of these styles could be applied to any form. A playwright might create a realistic comedy, or a romantic tragedy, or even perhaps an absurdist opera, incongruous as that seems.

These terms are simply signposts that refer us to historical patterns in form and style. To some extent, every play has its own form and style that is born of the unique personality of its playwright and of the culture in which its original theatre operated. It is virtually impossible to separate form and style from content.

Structural Form versus Tonal Form

Form can be described in terms of tone or of structure. Tone refers to the author's (and implicitly the audience's) attitude toward the experience of the play, its characters, and the overall world of the play. If it assumes a tragic or a comic pattern, the play accordingly becomes a tragedy or a comedy. Form is also a matter of structure. How the play defines its stage space and divides its stage time are formal matters governing structure. The fact that a play exists isolated in time and space means that the playwright must structure both these dimensions. **Structural form,** then, includes the way a play opens and closes, breaks its action into acts or scenes, and focuses its crucial moments. Both tonal and structural dimensions are ultimately determined by attitude. Bearing in mind that nothing in all this is fixed, it would be useful to examine the two sides of form, beginning with the structural side.

Historically, structural form has moved between two extremes: comprehensive and concentrated form (see p. 50.) **Comprehensive form** draws into the play's structure all the pertinent action of the natural story. It uses an early point of attack, thereby showing in action all the significant moments. To do so, it uses the stage as a neutral ground, easily becoming now one place, now another, or now one time, now another. Much medieval drama, Shakespearean and Elizabethan drama, and modern epic drama are all of this type. At the extreme opposite end of the spectrum is concentrated form. **Concentrated form** focuses all attention on the final, crucial moments of the natural story, accordingly employing a late point of attack and relying heavily on exposition to fill in earlier moments pertinent to the present. The stage in this case usually represents a particular locale more fully and retains the same scene throughout an act, if not the entire play. Classical, neoclassical, and realistic dramas tend toward this form.

Both forms have value. The comprehensive tends to engage the audience's imagination in order to fill out the theatrical illusion. The audience thus has a greater sense of collaborating in the play's creation. The concentrated tends to involve the audience's emotions more fully because it compacts the dramatic tension more tightly.

Structural form can also apply to the way a play divides its time into segments. By definition a play is itself a segment of time. It begins and therefore must end. The initial impression and the "parting shot" are both structural matters of great importance. So too are any curtains or blackouts that may occur during the course of the play. Each act or scene thus created is a formal unit of the overall structure. Various formal considerations derive from the one-act play structure as opposed to a multiact or full-length structure. For several centuries, the five-act structure was regarded as essential. For much of the twentieth century, the three-act play was the norm, recently replaced by the two-act structure. Overall length has been determined by various extrinsic factors over the years as well. The ancient Greeks had a stamina unknown to us and indulged in an entire day of tragedies presented in the form of a trilogy, three plays unified usually by theme or story line. Broadway prefers plays that end before the trains to the suburbs stop running. Still, audiences are not accustomed nowadays to enduring a play over three hours long. Occasionally, enduring a marathon session is a fashionable thing to do, as in the case of Eugene O'Neill's nine-act *Strange Interlude* or the more recent *Nicholas Nickleby,* based on Charles Dickens's work and presented by the Royal Shakespeare Company. These are expectations made possible by the enormity of the prestige of those producing them.

Tonal form is closely tied to tradition and audience expectation. The attitude of the playwright, which he or she of course hopes to inspire in the audience as well, leads to patterns that shape the play. Some traditional forms have taken the dominant tones to the logical, structural conclusion, creating tragedy, tragicomedy, comedy, farce, melodrama, and so forth. These traditional forms demonstrate the relationship between attitude and form and provide options always worth considering.

Historically, tonal form has moved between two extremes, much as has structural form. At one extreme is the doctrine of **fixed form** and at the other extreme, **organic form.** The doctrine of fixed form holds that a play must adhere to a definite pattern partly because it renders the play accessible to audiences and partly because there is an innate beauty, challenge, and appealing purity in formality. The doctrine of organic form holds that a play must assume the form uniquely suited to it and that there should be no definite, fixed forms. The truth lies somewhere between these doctrines. Inasmuch as no play can avoid coming to terms with its audience, it must adhere in some measure to audience expectations and hence traditional form. On the other hand, every play is its own experience, free to lay down its own terms, and audiences tend to grant that license to the playwright, at least up to the point at which they can continue to enter into the world of the play.

Currently, few hold much conviction in the doctrine of fixed form. It had its day during the seventeenth century, when only two forms of drama were regarded as legitimate: comedy and tragedy, each of which had fixed and pure features. Nowadays, the world has begun to strike us as so baffling that no form can adequately express our responses. Certainly, no good rationale for purity of form remains. Contemporary plays often employ a provocative and ironic mixture of tones, leaving audiences both amused and horrified, delighted and mystified, or charmed and awed. Still, the implications behind standard forms passed down through the ages are worth exploring. They tell us a great deal about how attitude, empathy, and emotional response all tend to create patterns in drama. A play, we need to remind ourselves, is an artifice contrived to attain effectiveness through engaging our response. Form is a deliberate means to that end.

Linear, Montage, and Circular Structures

What determines a play's structure is the manner in which its events are linked in the progression of action. Linkage may develop by causation, one event causing the next to occur—a logical movement that keeps the audience engaged through anticipation of each cause and effect. **Linear structure,** probably the most common, moves forward in a direct line. Naturally, it encourages a tight and compelling plot. A long-standing tradition stands behind this structure: we find it used in ancient Greek plays, in French neoclassical plays, in nineteenth-century "Well-Made" Plays, and in most modern realistic plays. Sophocles' *Oedipus Rex*, Jean Racine's *Phaedra*, Alexandre Dumas *fils' Camille*, Henrik Ibsen's *Hedda Gabler,* and Sam Shepard's *Buried Child* are all examples, despite their strong differences.

One alternative to this sort of structure stresses context, the nesting of each event, as much as it does linkage. **Montage structure** works by juxtaposing one event against another, not by a necessary cause and effect but rather by a deliberate contrast, much as the cinema derives effect from the alternation of shots, also called montage. Montage tends to encourage an episodic structure composed of multiple scenes occurring in widely disparate times or places. One scene tends to undercut or contrast the last one. Just as linear structure leans toward concentrated dramaturgy, montage structure leans toward comprehensive dramaturgy, found in Elizabethan plays, epic theatre, and some postmodern plays. Examples might include Shakespeare's *A Midsummer Night's Dream*, Bertolt Brecht's *Caucasian Chalk Circle,* and Heiner Müller's *Hamletmachine.*

The third structure, **circular structure,** has some kinship with montage, but rather than depending on juxtaposition for effect it depends on rounding the experience through a spirit of discovery that leads into various avenues. Circular structure has the tendency to work more through parallelism and association rather than through contrast in linking one event to another. We find it used in much medieval drama, which often depicts events seen from several points of view, events that strike a parallel to a previous one, or events presented as a series of stations in a journey of discovery, as in some of the cycle plays presenting the biblical story or in morality plays such as *Everyman.* Circular structure is also associated with expressionistic drama, as in Georg Kaiser's *From Morn to Midnight.* It has reappeared in postmodern theatre and especially in feminist theatre, as in the case of Maria Irene Fornes's *Fefu and Her Friends* or Paula Vogel's *How I Learned to Drive.*

Traditional Tonal Forms

Putting aside the many special forms of theatre such as opera, ballad opera, operetta, musical comedy, dance drama, musical review, and so forth, the drama encompasses three basic tonal forms: tragedy, comedy, and tragicomedy. These tonal forms are related directly to mood, attitude, or tone and can cut across the special theatre forms, applying equally well to musical or dance forms as to the so-called legitimate theatre. Each of the three has its subforms and variations, and each has assumed new patterns with each succeeding age, but they remain identifiable by tone. The tone is evident in the emotional response the piece seeks to create. **Tragedy** tends to arouse a sense of awe and wonder in the face of the seriousness and universality of the suffering at the center of the spectacle—what Aristotle called pity and fear. Melodrama is a variation on the tragic mood, creating an alternation of fear, indignation, and relief. **Comedy** arouses amusement at the absurdities and human vagaries that make up its spectacle. It relies on incongruities, the sense that things are somehow out of joint, and it usually resolves in a spirit of camaraderie. Farce is a variation, emphasizing physical buffoonery and outrageous exaggeration. **Tragicomedy** is a mixed form, calling for a certain controlled ambiguity of tone. It is the most common form in the modern theatre, perhaps because of the ambiguity of modern life.

Of the various tonal forms, tragedy is the most fixed, the most traditional, for it is held in such high esteem—so much so that the dramatic counterpart to the challenge of writing the Great American Novel is that of composing a Modern Tragedy. Somehow, by definition a tragedy is expected to be great. So few are written in the contemporary theatre that to write one at all would be remarkable. Actually, the problem here is that tragedy has become as much a value judgment as it is a distinct form. If we put aside the values connoted by the term "tragedy," the form is not so unusual after all.

Tragedy seeks to excite empathetic awe at the spectacle of a human being (or beings) face to face with the most threatening and challenging circumstances that life can entail. The human condition does entail threats and challenges we normally shy away from, those too dire for us to wish to face. Nevertheless, they intrigue us and pique our curiosity. In the relative safety of the theatre, we can vent that curiosity at no expense to our personal security. The spectacle itself and our response to it can enlarge our awareness of the conditions of the life we lead. This purpose implies a series of characteristics.

Tragedy is usually structured around a single protagonist, a person strong enough to meet the challenges implied but weak enough for us to identify with as a fellow human being. The challenge is both urgent and dire. If not surmounted, it poses grave dangers not only to the individual but frequently also to those associated with him or her, if not society at large. The source of the challenge is not trivial. It might derive from fate, an error in judgment, another character, or—usually—from all three. In some ironic way, the protagonist actually collaborates in bringing this threat or challenge to the surface. In any event, the play's progress moves from relative calm and contentment to catastrophe. Whether the protagonist survives or not, the test has been dire. Often there is a sense of an emerging new order at the end of the play. Tragedy presents the spectacle of humanity confronting the worst life can offer and, in the act of confronting it, assuming a dignity that is not lost even if the protagonist must succumb.

The audience of a tragedy undergoes an emotional release, which Aristotle labeled "catharsis": an unleashing of our deep-seated, suppressed fears through the vicarious experience of the play. He defined tragedy's focus to be pity and fear, the emotions that the form arouses and expends on "a worthy subject," the protagonist being someone better than the average, yet fully human.

These are the traditional characteristics of tragedy. The great tragedies of the past, especially those of the Greeks and of Shakespeare in the Elizabethan age, have become the models, rightly or wrongly. These tragedies pit the protagonist against the gods or against the forces of the cosmos, and they assume grandeur through the magnitude of the confrontation and the loftiness of their style. Although *Oedipus Rex* and *Hamlet* may be considered quintessential tragedies, many other plays certainly qualify as tragedies, even some from the contemporary theatre, plays such as Brecht's *Mother Courage*, Pirandello's *Henry IV*, Miller's *The Crucible*, and Dürrenmatt's *The Visit* (even if he preferred to call it "grotesque comedy").

Although a variation on tragedy, melodrama carries a negative connotation. This term is sometimes applied to plays that might be considered tragedies if only they were better plays. If tragedy is made trivial and if it ends happily with virtue triumphant, the result is "mere melodrama." We tend to think of the melodramatic as synonymous with the sensational. There may be good reasons for this, but remember that the term is only a category, not a value.

The essence of melodrama lies in its spectacle of disaster. Like tragedy it deals with dire threats and challenges, but these are produced now by forces outside the protagonist. They result from some hidden offstage force or from the machinations of an evil antagonist; there is no ironic collaboration between fate and the protagonist. Events tend to happen of their own accord, without the protagonist having decided to take a step toward disaster. For this reason, villains abound in melodrama.

All this suggests that melodrama generally contains less substance than tragedy. This is true. On the other hand, melodrama is well suited to certain sorts of human experience. All of us face the chance of sudden disaster or of being victimized. Circumstances completely beyond our control that drastically alter our lives do occur. If the emphasis is placed on the human response to disaster, a melodrama can be fully meaningful. Moreover, melodrama is inherently theatrical, producing strong tension and spectacular effects. Some excellent plays fit this description: Harold Pinter's *The Birthday Party*, Charles Gordone's *No Place to Be Somebody*, and Friedrich Dürrenmatt's *The Physicists* (which he again would call a grotesque comedy). If emphasis is placed instead on the disaster itself, as in many nineteenth-century melodramas such as Dion Boucicault's *The Octoroon*, or in present-day disaster films such as *Airport* or *Jaws*, the drama suffers a loss of substance even while gaining high spectacle. These are the works that give melodrama its bad name.

Comedy depends on the creation of the ludicrous, in the broadest sense of the word, by developing spectacles of incongruity, deliberate inconsistency, and absurdity. One way or another characters are caught up in circumstances beyond their control, but the emphasis this time is on the laughable. This means that the circumstances must be more discomfiting than dire. Laughing is both a mysterious and a peculiarly human activity. Why we do it, nobody quite knows. We can point to the sorts of things that provoke laughter even though we cannot explain it. As Henri Bergson indicates in his essay "On Laughter," we tend to laugh at the spectacle of mechanical or inelastic behavior. Any sort of behavior that cannot adjust to a new circumstance because of its own rigidity can be laughable. Adaptability is one of humanity's better traits. Society seeks to maintain such flexibility by ridiculing those who refuse to adapt or cannot. Another way to look at the human capacity for laughter is to recognize that we human beings, each and every one of us, have weaknesses that we all like to indulge but in our wisdom do not. We derive amusement in the theatre from witnessing others indulge them and letting them suffer the consequences. There are of course varieties of laughter. The amount of laughter produced, as measured, say, on a laugh meter, is no gauge of the quality of a comedy. Laughter can be an inward amusement or an outward guffaw. Likewise, the source can range from gentle humor to bitter satire. All of these types of laughter tend to portray humanity as caught up in absurd or incongruous situations that defy rational analysis.

Comedy encompasses a great many subforms: situation comedy, comedy of character, comedy of ideas, comedy of manners (or high comedy), and just plain farce (or low comedy). Farce is the most extreme form of comedy. It relies on physical spectacle. The contrast between the exalted notions we have of our human glory and the mundane necessities to which we must submit provides the grist for the farcical mill. For all our dignity, we still occupy physical bodies, farce reminds us. For example, the man of great purpose and dignity who steps on a banana peal or the man of amiable good nature who gets a pie in the face are old surefire farcical pieces of business.

Other forms of comedy rely on the sight of human beings caught in suddenly discomfiting circumstances, but they do so on different levels and with greater subtlety. Situation comedy pits relatively normal human beings against absurd situations. Comedy of character pits absurd characters against situations that would ordinarily seem normal. Comedy of ideas tends to construct whole worlds out of topsy-turvy ideas and values, which prove as valid as the counterparts we so thoroughly believe in in our world. Finally, comedy of manners pits pretentious characters against more knowledgeable ones who usually do the discomfiting.

Whatever the form, comedy concentrates on the incongruous, producing pain for the characters, but pain that is not strong enough or permanent enough to interfere with our recognition of the ridiculous. It has the effect of making us feel for the moment just a little superior. In order to do so, comedy virtually demands characters who take themselves and their circumstances very seriously. The character who thinks he is funny, and his playwright who knows he is, are both doomed to failure.

Because it is a mixed form, tragicomedy does not allow as precise a description as comedy and tragedy. Its form is correspondingly more organic, altering more radically from one play to another. What perhaps most clearly marks it is a controlled ambiguity of tone. In the case of a bad play, there is first and foremost an ambiguity of tone. We simply do not know what to make of the play. Are we supposed to take it seriously? What is this all about, anyway? But in the case of tragicomedy, this ambiguity is carefully controlled. Indeed, it is a source of dramatic tension. A single event may strike a provocative balance between the humorous and the pathetic, or between the whimsical and the tragic. We feel both reactions and hesitate to give full vent to either one. These plays may give enormous comic pleasure from time to time and yet bring us up short as we recognize that what we laughed about is altogether too serious and threatening for laughter. Tragicomedy is perhaps the most favored dramatic form in the present age because we perceive our own world with a similar ambiguity: Things are simultaneously absurd and out of joint even as they threaten our very existence. Some fine examples of the tragicomic form include Chekhov's *The Three Sisters,* Pirandello's *Six Characters in Search of an Author,* Stoppard's *Rosencrantz and Guildenstern Are Dead,* Beckett's *Waiting for Godot,* and David Storey's *Home.*

Tragedy, melodrama, comedy, farce, and tragicomedy are the major traditional dramatic forms. They are by no means fixed, especially today. Classification has become progressively difficult as playwrights shape more and more forms to suit their particular plays. Chekhov was fond of calling his plays comedies, whereas his director Constantin Stanislavski called them tragedies, and here at least one of them *(The Three Sisters)* has been called tragicomedy. Dürrenmatt called his plays "grotesque comedies," whereas here one *(The Visit)* has been called a tragedy and another *(The Physicists)* called a melodrama. Even a modern tragedy is apt to produce a healthy dose of laughter and amusement, and a modern comedy often generates moments of sudden horror or amazement. Still, the traditional forms can tell us something about how tone influences form.

Style and the World of the Play

A play occupies its own world. The playwright reigns over that world, determining the conditions that govern the characters who inhabit it. As we have seen, that is what allows special internal probability to operate—the fact that the play's world is not the real world. In that godlike stance, the playwright has license to shape circumstances any way he or she pleases. This is not a matter of exercising pure whimsy. Decisions are derived from a combination of the attitude the playwright takes toward the material and the perspective or point of view he or she adopts. The former has to do with form, the latter with style. It is difficult to make an absolute distinction between the two. A playwright's style tends to merge with his or her form. In fact, a proclivity for a certain form is part of a particular style. Style is particularly difficult to define with any precision. In simplest terms, it is a characteristic mode of expression rooted in the way a person views reality. Because it is in the nature of any piece of art to allow its creator to alter the conditions of actual life, we would expect the artist to do so in accordance with a personal vision.

The real world does not make decisions about style. Nothing is necessarily more important than anything else as far as nature is concerned. But for us, some things matter very much. Style is a reflection of that concern. We care very much about death, for example, indifferent as nature may be. Because it is human nature to care, a play (which really is an expression of care) naturally takes on a certain coloration reflecting that care. Form too is the product of care, but in the case of style it appears chiefly in the treatment, the quality and color of the action. This is a continual reminder that there is a consciousness and a sensibility behind what we witness on the stage. A playwright maintains a presence through the style and coherence of the play's world. Even an absurdist, believing the world empty and devoid of meaning and value, writes plays out of care, out of concern for the agony that that emptiness produces in us human beings who so need meaning.

Theatre is an act of communication. A play restructures the world using living beings encountering one another in three-dimensional space. And as they encounter the audience, the theatre experience produces a shared vision. Our view of the world merges momentarily with that of the play. Dissimilar as our individual views of reality may be, we agree on enough points to make theatre possible. We disagree enough that it is virtually impossible for any two people to write the same play, even if they agree beforehand on the plot, characters, and setting. Human uniqueness is the source of style.

In any form of expression, the same principle operates. The Sunday comics are a potpourri of styles. Cathy's world is sharply different from Dr. Morgan's, whose world could never be confused with Blondie's, nor hers with that of Dennis the Menace. Each artist uses the same formal elements in creating the comic strip, but the viewpoints, sensibilities, and manners of expression vary enormously. Each artist has worked long enough with his or her material that every element has taken a comfortable place in the world of the strip, and we cannot help but share a little of that world. In the theatre, the encounter is so much richer, so much more immediate, that our engagement with the world of the play can be very strong.

A playwright is constantly designing new worlds, one for each play. Although many stylistic qualities carry over, they still have to be reestablished at the outset of each new play. When we encounter a play, we look at once for any insights into the nature of this new world. What sorts of things are apt to happen here? How are they apt to happen? Style is a code giving us some insight. The world of the play becomes more or less coherent and believable in direct ratio to how authoritative its style is. The stage must become its own world. We must believe not only that it has every right to be there, but also that it could be no other way, at least for the time being. When that happens, style is present.

Personal versus Established Style

Style can be said to be the social dimension of theatre. It develops as a means of sharing a vision of reality. Such visions vary not only from one individual to another but also from one culture to another. One is the source of personal style, the other of established style. They are not mutually exclusive. A personal style operates within an established style. Shakespeare shared many stylistic qualities with other Elizabethan playwrights and yet there are elements that make his plays distinctly his.

Established style has usually held sway throughout an entire age, receding only as a new view of reality comes to supplant it, thereby calling for a new style. An ancient Greek, an eighteenth-century Japanese, and a modern American obviously would not see reality the same way: Sophocles' *Oedipus Rex*, Takeda Izumo's Kabuki play *Chushingura*, and Tennessee Williams's *The Glass Menagerie* testify to that. Doubtless, *The Glass Menagerie* would strike Takedo Izumo as strange, fully as strange as his play would strike Sophocles. The reason is that the plays are based on views of reality alien to each other. The more alien the play, the more apparent the stage's contrivance. It reminds us yet again that the stage is fundamentally all pretense. As such, its ability to reflect reality depends on whether the audience can read a reality in the complex of pretenses. For most of us Westerners, Kabuki's illusions do not work because, not sharing the Kabuki view of reality, we cannot understand the stage conventions it produced.

Through the ages, reality has been perceived in ever-changing ways. In response, theatre has constantly developed new styles. Until recently, such styles generally endured for more than a century. Neoclassicism, for example, emerged out of the Italian Renaissance and became a rather fixed style in France after the 1630s. It continued as an accepted style through virtually all of the eighteenth century. For that long a period, the style corresponded to accepted ideas of the nature of the world and the sort of theatre that could best reflect it. Since the late nineteenth century, however, there has been no such unanimity about the nature of the world. Truth has become more and more relative. A proliferation of styles has accompanied this development. The twentieth century has been aptly called the age of "isms." The period did indeed witness a cavalcade of styles: realism, naturalism, symbolism, expressionism, futurism, dada, surrealism, epic theatre, theatre of the absurd, theatre of cruelty, the happening, environmental theatre, total theatre, postmodernism, and so forth. These are established styles. The array might also seem akin to the Tower of Babel, compounded as it is by the myriad styles we have inherited from the past and witnessed in revivals of centuries-old plays. In very general terms, we can define the dominant styles we are most apt to encounter in the theatre. The following sections provide a descriptive catalog.

Greek Drama

The Greeks of the fifth century B.C. saw life as governed by irrational forces embodied in the various gods. Human beings are subject to the whims of the gods. The universe is neither benign nor malignant, but it does revolve around humankind. The gods take an interest in us and manipulate us. Accordingly, fate plays a major part in theatrical spectacle, whether it be comic or tragic. In the case of tragedy, the protagonist faces enormous odds that would daunt any ordinary mortal, and we watch his or her struggle in tandem with a chorus that is both audience and participant. The style reduces action and character to essential qualities, providing a sense of simple dignity. In the case of comedy, the main characters engage in clever games in order to outwit fate, often conjuring some absurd scheme to solve a huge problem such as war, debt, death, taxation, or sex. Again we join a chorus, but this time they may be curious creatures such as birds or frogs. The same tendency toward simplicity now creates buffoons of the characters. Examples include, for tragedy, Aeschylus's *Agamemnon*, Sophocles's *Oedipus Rex*, and Euripides' *Medea*, and for comedy, Aristophanes' *Lysistrata*.

Roman Drama

Most of what we have in the way of Roman drama are the comedies of Plautus and Terence, dating from the third into the second centuries B.C. These plays are characterized by a greater realism in that the action almost always transpires among ordinary, though exaggerated, townspeople meeting on a city street. The chorus is gone now and the action engages us through madcap physical activity motivated by mistakes, confused identities, and misunderstandings. The style derives from a view of humanity as controlled by base instincts, especially hunger and sex. What little we know of tragedy, illustrated by the plays of Seneca of the first century A.D., suggests that the view of humanity is substantially the same, but now manifested in horrendous blood letting, revenge, and outright cruelty. Examples are Plautus's *Manaechmi* and Terence's *Andria* for comedy and Seneca's *Phaedra* for tragedy.

Medieval Drama

The plays of the fourteenth through the sixteenth centuries were by and large based on the stories of the Bible, and yet they tended to be anachronistic, portraying biblical characters as contemporary shepherds or kings or tax collectors. The worldview placed humanity in a middle ground between heaven and hell and subject to the heavy burdens of this vale of tears and yet promised the chance of salvation through the redeeming grace of Christ. Time is split between earthly progression toward death and heavenly all-encompassing time, in which God sees all time in one time. This helps account for the anachronisms. The plays, then, use the stage as a relatively neutral space defined and redefined by specific but suggestive scenic units (mansions) placed between heaven and hell. The style uses parallels between the exalted and the mundane, between the heavenly and the earthly or everyday. Tone is mixed in these plays, alternating between the reverent and the farcical. Examples include *The Second Shepherds' Play* and *Everyman.*

Elizabethan and Spanish Golden Age Drama

From the late sixteenth century through most of the seventeenth century, drama in England and Spain tended to share a style that derived from a vision of humanity as being at the center of an essentially benevolent universe but caught up in the human weaknesses of overweening pride, self-indulgence, power mongering, or pure, self-serving viciousness. These weaknesses break our bond with God and thwart our duty to maintain the natural peace and order He had ordained. The world in these plays is represented on a bare stage that can be transformed from one place and time to another according to the action played on it. The stage becomes the earthly ground on which the mundane actions of mere human beings is set against our awareness of a divine and caring spirit watching over us, located in the "heavens," the roofed attic space set above the stage in the Elizabethan playhouse. In the absence of full illusion of time and place, the style depends on language, metaphor, and allusion to play on the audience's imagination. Examples include William Shakespeare's *King Lear* and Lope de Vega's *Fuente Ovejuna* (or *The Sheep Well*).

Renaissance Drama and Neoclassicism

Meanwhile, in Italy and France drama took a different direction from the sixteenth through most of the eighteenth centuries. Inspired by discoveries of the ancient works of Greece and Rome, first the Italians and then the French attempted to revive the glory of classical drama. The result is a mutation called "neoclassicism." Its style is intensely rational, based on the concept of verisimilitude, which literally means "likeness to truth." This concept dictated that the stage be used to present the essence of human experience. Nothing impossible in reality should be represented on stage. No abnormalities or idiosyncracies should appear, as they detract from the essential nature of our lives. Plays must therefore be closely unified. They were written to transpire in a span of time no longer than one day, within the same general locale and without any detracting subplots. The unities of time, place, and action helped ensure focus on the essence of experience. Style is characterized by an extreme economy, so that the plays are highly concentrated in structure. The style also calls for purity of tone: Comedy must constitute laughable exposure of human foibles and tragedy the horrors of mistaken judgment. Examples include Niccolò Machiavelli's *The Mandrake* (or *La Mandragola*), Jean Racine's *Phaedra*, and Molière's *Tartuffe*.

Romanticism

In reaction to the extreme rationalism of the neoclassicists, a new emphasis developed on human intuition. Toward the end of the eighteenth century, this led to plays that were much less formal and unified. Instead, they were expressions of the creative artist's unique, personal vision, informed by an instinctual sense for truth that transcended rational thought. Accordingly, freedom was exalted and artists felt free to explore their created worlds unrestricted by rules and regulations. Even the physical limitations of the stage did not inhibit their creative endeavors, with the result that many romantic plays are unstageable. Even when stageable, the settings called for are elaborate, rich, and painterly. In similar spirit, romanticism tends to celebrate the natural and even the esoteric, placing the action in remote worlds removed from civilization. The plays are often set in strange and unusual locales: deep, dark grottoes; medieval castles; or among the natives of distant lands. Characters are caught up in battles for freedom or subject to strange and mysterious forces. Examples are Johann Wolfgang von Goethe's *Faust, Parts I* and *II*, Friedrich von Schiller's *Wilhelm Tell*, and Victor Hugo's *Hernani*.

Realism

Romanticism inspired in turn another reaction. In place of the romantics' sweeping celebration of the creative spirit, the realists sought to portray life through closely duplicating the appearance of the actual world we observe around us. The style plays on the objective experience of the senses, trying faithfully to reproduce the way we see and hear real life. The style grows out of the positivist conviction that only directly observable experience is reliable as a way of knowing. Accordingly, it tends to place the action within the proscenium arch, with the characters behaving as though the audience were not there. On the other hand, realistic playwrights, unlike naturalistic playwrights, do work to shape effects, give emphasis, and add tone to the action. Realism tends toward concentrated dramatic action, one act of a play lasting as long as the action portrayed. It consequently depends heavily on reporting previous events and events taking place beyond the confines of the stage. Realism began as a conscious movement in the 1870s and continues today. Examples include Henrik Ibsen's *A Doll's House* (1879), Anton Chekhov's *The Cherry Orchard* (1904), George Bernard Shaw's *Major Barbara* (1907), Sean O'Casey's *Juno and the Paycock* (1924), Clifford Odets's *Awake and Sing!* (1937), Eugene O'Neill's *Moon for the Misbegotten* (1943), Jason Miller's *That Championship Season* (1975), Marsha Norman's *'night, Mother* (1983), and August Wilson's *Fences* (1987).

Naturalism

Naturalism is an extreme form of realism that emerged at about the same time and grew out of a desire to turn theatre into a science. The naturalists wanted to use the theatre as a laboratory to investigate social and psychological issues. The playwright must operate, they insisted, as a detached observer, much as a scientist examines an experiment in progress. Events in a play should develop naturally out of the conditions laid down. Thus, everything must be a rigorous duplication of real life, down to the most minute details, causing naturalist plays to be called "slices of life." The fourth wall must be strictly maintained as we watch life being lived by characters who have no notion that they are on stage in our view. Moreover, their "room" should be a box set because rooms in real life have right-angled corners. Unlike realistic plays, no attempt is made to lay emphasis on any one factor. Naturalism was a short-lived movement, lasting from about 1880 to 1910. Examples include Émile Zola's *Thérèse Raquin* (1873), Henri Becque's *The Vultures* (1882), August Strindberg's *Miss Julie* (1888), Gerhardt Hauptmann's *The Weavers* (1892), and Maxim Gorki's *The Lower Depths* (1902).

Symbolism

Sometimes called "neoromanticism," symbolism called for a return to romanticism's celebration of instinct or intuition. The symbolists objected to the reliance of realism and naturalism on objective reality, arguing that to do so gives us only the appearance of things, not a glimpse of the deeper reality we can have only through the power of symbol and suggestion. Accordingly, symbolism as a style places a strong emphasis on atmosphere created by light and shadow, misty and mystical images, and dreamlike evanescence. Typically, the audience experiences the sensation of being transported out of our mundane, physical world into a dreamlike realm imbued with silence or rhythmic sounds and diffused light. The darkening of the auditorium and the mesmerizing effect of the play of lights on stage all support this effect. The movement is closely associated with the symbolist poets of Paris who published their views in a manifesto of 1885 and from then on depended on Stephane Mallarmé as their major spokesman. This too was a short-lived movement, lasting from about 1890 to 1915. Nevertheless, it continued through modifications in the New Stagecraft and in later movements such as futurism, dada, and surrealism. It is also closely associated with the art-for-art's sake movement in England led by Walter Pater. Examples are Maurice Maeterlinck's *The Intruder* (1890) and *Pelléas and Mélisande* (1892), Oscar Wilde's *Salomé* (1893), Gabriele d'Annunzio's *The Dead City* (1898), John Millington Synge's *Riders to the Sea* (1904), and Leonid Andreyev's *The Life of Man* (1907).

Expressionism

Expressionism is an extreme form of symbolism that presents a personal dream rather than the universal dream sought by the earlier symbolists. As a style, it attempts to reproduce the devices and effects of actual dreams, including distortions, telescoping of time, omission of some details while enlarging others, shifting identities of characters, skewing of objects, enlargement or diminishment of natural proportions, and places that transform into new places. Expressionist plays give the audience the impression of having entered the head of the dreamer, the playwright. Expressionism also tends to be more programmatic than symbolism, exalting the nobility of the human soul, which is depicted as being dragged down by the physical, animalistic, suffocating reality of human existence (in the case of "mystical" expressionism) or by the inhumane forces of society, such as political power, money, industry, and militarism (in the case of "activist" expressionism). In either case, deliberate distortion of objective reality is the key element. The style first appeared at the turn of the twentieth century, and it became a conscious movement around 1912 and lasted until 1930. Examples include such mystical expressionist plays as August Strindberg's *The Dream Play* (1902) and *The Ghost Sonata* (1907), Frank Wedekind's *Pandora's Box* (1904), and Eugene O'Neill's *The Emperor Jones* (1921), and activist expressionist plays such as Georg Kaiser's *From Morn to Midnight* (1916) and Ernst Toller's *Man and the Masses* (1921).

Existentialist Drama

Existentialist drama grew out of mystical expressionism but dispensed with its insistence on dreamlike distortion and highly personal visions. Existentialism is also not a conscious movement in quite the same way. It found its basis in the conviction that existence has no inherent meaning and yet humanity has an unquenchable desire for meaning, and it is strongly related to the philosophical views propounded by such people as Friedrich Nietzsche and Henri Bergson, both of whom described the disparity between life and the meaning humans attempt to impose on it. Translated into dramatic terms, the plays tend to derive dramatic tension from the dilemmas posed by the constant and inexorable movement of life and time set against the human effort to control life, shape it, and give it meaning. The effect is one of shifting realities, as though there were no one reality but instead many of them, depending on how we perceive the world around us. Both characters and audience find their convictions about what is real undermined by sudden new perceptions. Truth is therefore seen as relative, or, as Pirandello's play would have it, "right you are (if you think you are)." These plays also play on the disparity between one person's vision of himself or herself and the image thrown back by others. Awareness of the other is always an unsettling reminder of other truths. Existentialist drama had its beginnings with the writers of the *"teatro del grottesco,"* or the "theatre of the grotesque," in Italy and included such playwrights as Luigi Chiarelli, Pier Maria Rosso di San Secondo, Luigi Antonelli, and especially Luigi Pirandello. In France, early examples were associated with the *"théâtre de l'ine-sprimé,"* or the "theatre of the unexpressed," in the hands of such playwrights as Charles Vildrac, Jules Romains, and Henri-René Lenormand. Existentialist drama took on two slightly different expressions, one emphasizing the dilemma of defining existence (as in the plays of Pirandello, Camus, and Sartre) and the other depicting the sensation of separation from a removed and more meaningful realm (as in the plays of Jean Giraudoux, Jean Anouilh, Federico García Lorca, and Michel de Ghelderode). Examples include Luigi Pirandello's *Six Characters in Search of an Author* (1921) and *Henry IV* (1922), Jean Giraudoux's *Tiger at the Gates* (or *The Trojan War Shall Not Take Place*) (1935) and *Ondine* (1939), Jean Anouilh's *Antigone* (1943), Albert Camus's *Caligula* (1938), and Jean-Paul Sartre's *No Exit* (1944).

Epic Theatre

Epic theatre developed out of activist expressionism and the theatricalism of the stagings of such directors as Vsevolod Meyerhold in Russia and Erwin Piscator in Germany. It retains the spirit of activism from expressionism but discards the deliberate distortion of objective reality, substituting the "endistancing effect," the effect of making things strange (Brecht's term, translated from *Verfremdungseffekt*). Epic theatre is based on the conviction that society is the major force shaping our destinies, an enormously powerful force that works in collaboration with the mean-spirited and small-minded side of humanity. Implicitly, epic theatre argues that we in the audience can take action against such forces and emerge from the theatre determined to do battle against them. The world is portrayed with extreme economy that treats the stage as neutral ground and resorts to theatrical suggestion, never allowing thorough or sustained illusion. The stage is frankly a stage. It may represent now this locale, now that. Time may also be treated fluidly, representing years, even decades, within the span of a play. The spirit is essentially narrative ("epic") and the stage and the actors on it serve as mechanisms for storytelling. The settings are often in some way remote and strange, and the material often derives from history or legend. In later years, the material was often documentary and more recent, as in the case of the German "theatre of fact" practiced by Peter Weiss, Rolf Hochhuth, and Heinar Kipphardt. In any event, the effort is ultimately to draw a parallel between the strange world of the play and the familiar world of the audience. The style had its beginnings in the mid-twenties chiefly in the work of Bertolt Brecht, who was its initial spokesman. It continues today. Examples include Bertolt Brecht's *Mother Courage* (1938), *Galileo* (1939), and *Caucasian Chalk Circle* (1945); Friedrich Dürrenmatt's *The Visit* (1956); Max Frisch's *Biedermann and the Firebugs* (1958); John Arden's *Sergeant Musgrave's Dance* (1959); Dario Fo's *Isabella, Three Sailing Ships and a Con Man* (1963); Peter Weiss's *The Song of the Lusitanian Bogey* (1967); Arthur Kopit's

Indians (1969); Edward Bond's *Lear* (1971); and Tony Kushner's *Angels in America: The Milennium Approaches* (1992).

Modified Realism

Influenced by symbolism and expressionism, modified or psychological realism continued to rely on the presentation of life through objective detail and to play on the audience's senses of sight and sound, but it placed a different emphasis on the psychological drives that motivate human beings, thus introducing a subjective level. Frequently this subjectivity appears in the form of dreams, daydreams, reminiscences, or inner dialogue. Time is more fluid, and flashbacks, jumps forward in time, and telescoping of time are not uncommon. More than one locale might be represented on stage simultaneously, and in extreme cases the stage is rendered virtually bare so as to easily become a variety of places in either objective or subjective reality. Nevertheless, realistic details still root the spectacle in a real, objective, observable world. In short, the style is realistic modified by devices borrowed from expressionism and symbolism. The style first appeared in the 1920s, as in some of O'Neill's plays, but it did not take on momentum until the years following World War II, particularly in the United States. It is still in use today. Examples of modified realism include Tennessee Williams's *The Glass Menagerie* (1945), Arthur Miller's *Death of a Salesman* (1949), Peter Shaffer's *Equus* (1973), Milan Stitt's *The Runner Stumbles* (1975), and Brian Friel's *Dancing at Lughnasa* (1993.)

The Theatre of the Absurd

Theatre of the absurd is based on the conviction that the world is inherently meaningless and out of harmony with itself and with us. The theatre of the absurd attempts to characterize the stage in a deliberately chaotic manner and adopts a structure that assumes coherence only by building a climactic rhythm that eventually bursts the play's own bounds. Whereas existentialist drama explored characters confronted by meaninglessness, the theatre of the absurd transfers that confrontation to the audience. Frequently it works by encasing the characters in the confines of a proscenium stage, so that they appear stranded or cut off from what must really matter—something "out there." In extreme versions, the acts of entering and exiting correspond to birth and death. This style tends to rely on vivid physical images to create searing effects, such as corpses that grow, people who turn into rhinoceroses, old people consigned to ashcans, or a character who is gradually buried under sand or accumulating furniture. It has its inspiration in the term "absurd" as Camus uses it in his *Myth of Sisyphus*, where it refers to the sensation of emptiness, meaninglessness, and purposelessness, as if we were out of harmony with ourselves and life itself. The theatre of the absurd was centered mainly in Paris with the work of such playwrights as Eugène Ionesco, Samuel Beckett, Arthur Adamov, Fernando Arrabal, and Jean Genet. Nevertheless, it never has been a conscious movement with a program and manifestos. Instead, it is a phenomenon of the postwar period, a response to the horrors of war and the continued threat of nuclear annihilation.

Martin Esslin (1961) invented the term to describe these plays. Examples include Eugène Ionesco's *The Lesson* (1952) and *Rhinoceros* (1960), Samuel Beckett's *Waiting for Godot* (1953) and *Endgame* (1957), Jean Genet's *The Balcony* (1957), and Tom Stoppard's *Rosencrantz and Guildenstern Are Dead* (1967).

Allusive Realism

Allusive realism is closely allied to modified realism, but it replaces the emphasis on psychological motivations and subjective inner experience with allusions to forces at work beyond the characters. It remains essentially realistic in appearance, but it borrows from the theatre of the absurd some of its sense of a mysterious, powerful, but meaningless force operating beyond the bounds of objective reality. Typically, the play appears initially as a straightforward representation of a mundane world, but as it moves forward we become aware of strange or at least unseen forces. These forces are sometimes metaphysical, sometimes social, sometimes both. The characters and their worlds are suggestive of other things in our own world. Thus, the dramatic tension depends on our recognition of the allusions. These plays are often associated with existentialist thought and so represent alternations between levels of consciousness. They tend to treat characters as isolated and cut off, with powerful forces operating from beyond the confines of the stage. A variation on allusive realism is "magic realism," which does not present the objective world in fully realistic terms, but often deals with some outside, powerful, and supernatural force interfering with the mundane world. Examples of allusive realism include Harold Pinter's *Birthday Party* (1957) and *Homecoming* (1965), Slawomir Mrozek's *Tango* (1965), Václav Havel's *Largo Desolato* (1983), Peter Barnes's *The Ruling Class* (1969), John Guare's *House of Blue Leaves* (1970), Sam Shepard's *Buried Child* (1978) and *Fool for Love* (1983), David Mamet's *Glengarry Glen Ross* (1983,) Tom Stoppard's *Hapgood* (1991) and *Arcadia* (1994), and Michael Frayne's *Copenhagen* (1997). Examples of magic realism include Jose Rivera's *Marisol* (1994), Luigi Lunari's *Our Father* (1998), and Craig Lucas's *Prelude to a Kiss* (1991).

Postmodernism

Postmodernism is a style that evolved during the late 1970s and 1980s. It is based on extreme relativism ("contextual" relativism), which argues that there are no universals, no abiding truths, and that what is accepted as "truth" is governed by the power system of any given time (hegemony), dominant value systems, the immediate context, and individual perception. As a consequence, postmodern plays tend to splinter the action and focus, to throw things into juxtaposition without imposing a governing framework that implies meaning. Meaning is highly individual, and the postmodern playwright compiles a series of provocative scenes and images to play on the imagination and sensitivity of individual audience members. Plays tend to be highly reflexive, constantly calling attention to their stage devices and deliberately mixing media. Postmodernism also frequently uses well-known texts as pretexts for new plays. As a result, it is a style associated strongly with directors who develop plays through actors improvising the action and using the stage devices directly rather than scripting. The ideas of such people as Jacques Derrida and Michel Foucault are the basis of postmodernism. Examples are Heiner Müller's *Hamletmachine* (1977), Irene Maria Fornes's *The Conduct of Life* (1985), Elizabeth LeCompte's *Routes 1 & 9* (1981), and Robert Wilson's *the CIVIL warS* (1984).

All of these are recognized, established styles in the Western world. There are, of course, many more, but this list can serve as a convenient catalog that pinpoints the salient characteristics of each style. Note that different styles are generally associated with a particular span of time and often with a particular country or city.

Within established styles, individual dramatists have their personal styles. Recall the story of Harold Pinter's "weasel under the coffee table," a phrase that is vividly Pinteresque. As a way of illustrating personal style, following are three short scenes written in realistic style. As mentioned in the previous section on the realistic style, all of these plays employ every means to render the appearance and sound of the stage as much like the appearance and sound of the objective real world. To our eyes and ears, what happens on stage has the sense of everyday life. Of course, to do so these plays must resort to pretenses, such as a fourth wall that pretends to cut us off from the action, as though the characters were in one room and we in another. The scenes are nevertheless very different, each clearly written by a different dramatist. Indeed, the individual style is unmistakable. All three scenes are played out between a man and a woman, rendered here as nameless, simply "he" and "she." In each case, the characters have already developed expectations of each another. The scenes are parallel in this respect, and they share a sense of realism. If you know the playwrights at all, you will guess at once which scene is whose.

Scene 1

SHE: All these ten years I have believed in you so utterly—so utterly.

HE: You must go on believing in me!

SHE: Then let me see you stand free and high up!

HE: *(Sadly.)* Oh, it is not every day that I can do that.

SHE: *(Passionately.)* I will have you do it! I will have it! *(Imploringly.)* Just once more! Do the impossible once again!

HE: *(Stands and looks deep into her eyes.)* If I try it, I will stand up there and talk to Him as I did that time before.

SHE: *(In rising excitement.)* What will you say to Him?

HE: I will say to Him: Hear me, Mighty Lord—thou may'st judge me as seems best to thee. But hereafter I will build nothing but the loveliest thing in the world.

SHE: *(Carried away.)* Yes . . . yes . . . yes!

HE: . . . build it together with a princess, whom I love . . .

SHE: Yes, tell Him that! Tell Him that!

HE: Yes. And then I will say to Him: Now I shall go down and throw my arms round her and kiss her . . .

SHE: . . . many times! Say that!

HE: . . . many, many times, I will say.

SHE: And then?

HE: Then I will wave my hat . . . and come down to earth . . . and do as I said to Him.

Scene 2

SHE: You look ever so much nicer than when we last met. *(He looks up, surprised.)* What have you done to yourself?

HE: Washed; brushed; good night's sleep and breakfast. That's all.

SHE: Did you get back safely that morning?

HE: Quite, thanks.

SHE: Were they angry with you for running away from Sergius' charge?

HE: *(Grinning.)* No: they were glad; because they'd just run away themselves.

SHE: *(Going to the table, and leaning over it towards him.)* It must have made a lovely story for them: all that about me and my room.

HE: Capital story. But I only told it to one of them: a particular friend.

SHE: On whose discretion you could absolutely rely?

HE: Absolutely.

SHE: Hm! He told it all to my father and Sergius the day you exchanged the prisoners. (She turns away and strolls carelessly across to the other side of the room.)

HE: *(Deeply concerned and half incredulous.)* No! You don't mean that do you?

SHE: *(Turning, with sudden earnestness.)* I do indeed. But they don't know that it was in this house you took refuge. If Sergius knew, he would challenge you and kill you in a duel.

HE: Bless me! Then don't tell him.

SHE: Please be serious, Captain.

Again, this scene cuts off in midstream, but there is enough there to catch its style and flavor.

Scene 3

SHE: I'm so nervous, I'm worried. I went into service when I was quite a little girl, and now I'm not used to common life, and my hands are white, white as a lady's. I'm so tender and so delicate now, respectable and afraid of everything. . . . I'm so frightened. And I don't know what will happen to my nerves if you deceive me.

HE: *(Kisses her.)* Little cucumber! Of course, every girl must respect herself; there's nothing I dislike more than a badly behaved girl.

SHE: I'm awfully in love with you; you're educated, you can talk about everything. *(Pause.)*

HE: *(Yawns.)* Yes. I think this: if a girl loves anybody, then it means she's immoral. *(Pause.)* It's nice to smoke a cigar out in the open air. . . . *(Listens.)* Somebody's coming. It's the mistress, and people with her. *(She embraces him suddenly.)* Go to the house, as if you'd been bathing in the river: go by this path, or they'll meet you and will think I've been meeting you. I can't stand that sort of thing.

SHE: *(Coughs quietly.)* My head's aching because of your cigar.

The first scene is quoted from Henrik Ibsen's *The Master Builder,* a scene between Solness and Hilda. The second takes place between Captain Bluntschli and Raina in George Bernard Shaw's *Arms and the Man.* The last is from Anton Chekhov's *The Cherry Orchard,* a scene between the two servants Dunyasha and Yasha. All three plays are by now classics of the modern repertory. The characters behave in a fully realistic manner, as though the audience were not there and the characters occupied only the represented space: the large veranda of Solness's house, the library of Raina's father's house, and the garden of Mme. Ranevskaya's house, respectively. The three scenes portray life as we might witness it had we been there. Still, there is considerable difference in the styles.

What is sometimes most telling about a playwright's style is the dividing line between what is literally contained in the dialogue and action and what is implied. For example, the Hilda–Solness scene stresses an exultant striving pushed forward by Hilda's passionate encouragement. Implicit is a sense of overreaching and of impending doom. The Raina–Bluntschli scene is a word banter, in which what at first seems important gives way to something else. Implicit is the conviction that there is indeed something important underneath it all. Typically, Shaw works his scenes on the premise that what we may think is significant is insignificant, and vice versa. Finally, in Chekhov's case, the Dunyasha–Yasha scene is literally a love scene gone sour. Dunyasha gives direct expression of her feelings and witnesses her hopes curdle before her eyes. We feel both Yasha's blatant disdain and Dunyasha's private agony.

The decision to emphasize this or imply that aids more than anything in developing style. The stage cannot show us everything, nor would anyone want it to. Being shown everything would rob the play of its excitement. What the stage implies about the characters' lives is sometimes more fascinating than what it tells us directly. Implying something powerfully yet subtly can be one of a playwright's greatest gifts.

6 Steps in Analysis

What we should now be able to do is establish a series of steps that will yield a solid analysis of a play script. Such an analysis ought to be satisfying in and of itself as a way of understanding a script. Beyond that, it ought to be genuinely useful in the process of staging a play. Moving from page to stage means that the director, actors, and designers have a solid idea of what is on the page before they take it to the stage. We have laid down sufficient groundwork to know what we are looking for. Now we apply these principles to the actual task of analyzing the script in order to discover the sources of tension and how they are organized and then to distill the evidence in order to present a coherent analysis. This calls for at least three readings of the script, each with a distinct purpose. In all three readings, we have to experience the play that is implicit in the script—we need to read with a theatre in our head. That means we have to be alert to all the sources of effect that the stage medium affords and be constantly alive to the way this particular script taps into them. Vertical analysis is an aid to doing just that.

Vertical versus Horizontal Analysis

Vertical analysis forces us to recognize that a play accumulates effects. At certain moments, we come to sense an effect. We can then assess what contributes to that effect. The playwright will have shaped it by manipulating the stage medium: its space, the relationship of characters, their motivations, the contrast with a previous moment, the sense of time past or of other places, or any number of other sources outlined previously. The combination of sources is in constant flux. One moment may tap one set of sources, the next a different set. The combination is never the same.

In horizontal analysis, probably the most commonly used approach, plot dominates. Such analysis holds that plot is fundamental to a play's structure and so should be analyzed first. After that, other elements are traced throughout the duration of the play. To do this, we might, for example, resort to the six Aristotelian elements: plot, character, thought, language, music, and spectacle. Then we follow each of these strands throughout the play. How is plot being used? How are events linked? Where are the major discoveries and reversals? Then we turn to character. How do we know the characters? What sorts of things do we know and what sorts don't we know about them? Then on the subject of thought, we look for meaning, the thematic content inherent in the play's experience. Having done that, we take the matter down to the level of performance by looking at the uses of language, with its allusions, symbolism, and references, then at the rhythms and tempos employed, and finally at the uses of spectacle: scenery, costumes, lights, sound, and so forth.

All of these matters do indeed demand our attention; they are all pertinent. The problem with horizontal analysis is that it breaks the play into strands lasting throughout the length of the play and leaves us without a sense of the whole. It provides no way of unifying the strands once separated and examined. Such analysis also tends to discourage us from looking at the audience as a living and powerful ingredient in the mix. After all, we do not experience a play in strands; we experience it moment by moment. These moments, realized as action that coheres to produce effect, deserve our attention. This is the essence of vertical analysis.

In vertical analysis, we start by breaking down the play into its most significant phases, sequences that culminate in an effect on the audience. Each organic segment plays on one set of tensions made palpable to us through selective use of stage elements. These segments build on one another to create an effect, forming a meaningful sequence. The play as a whole is built out of these landmark moments. By isolating these landmarks, we can locate the stage elements that contribute to the effect. In one instance, the effect might derive largely from a twist in the plot, but at another it might depend much more heavily on scenery, or on a character insight, or on a sound, or any number of things. Stage elements can come together in all sorts of combinations. We concentrate on the telling moments in the play and look for the ways in which they are shaped, never losing sight of the audience. In short, vertical analysis lets us analyze on the basis of the experience we will have as the play happens.

Three Fundamental Questions

When we undertake the analysis of a particular script, we ought first to remind ourselves of some fundamental matters that can help us know what we are looking for. First, every play is distinct from actuality. It would be impossible, in any event, to duplicate a real-life experience on stage. The minute any experience is isolated for our view, it alters from its natural state. Once isolated, the human experience must be made palpable to an audience in stage terms, making it "stageworthy." The script is the playwright's blueprint for the realization of the play on stage before an audience. As such, the script consists of the playwright's manipulations. What we are looking for in the first instance are the signs of manipulation. So the first of three questions we are attempting to answer is: "How is this play different from actuality?" We should be able to find signs of manipulation in the pattern of tensions.

The second matter worth remembering is that a play separates itself from actuality in order to reflect on human experience. Plays are not just constructs and analysis is not just discovering structure. Ultimately, the most important element in a play is its audience—as mentioned earlier, a play is not a play until it has an audience. The pattern of tensions we discover in answering the first question is there for a purpose. All the manipulation is intended to create an effect on the audience. Effects accumulate all the way through the play up to the final parting effect as the curtain falls and the lights fade. Having found out how the play is different from actuality, our second question is: "Why is the play different in this way?" Theoretically, the play is different in this way because it creates effect by being so. We must not forget that a play is an experience, not an essay or a lecture, but some sort of human life set before us. We may find humor in it. We may find it awesome and thrilling. We may see pathos and suffering and even share in it a little.

Finally, we must remind ourselves that plays have content. They are not empty. The accumulation of effects leads us to recognize something about the human experience. This is true even of the most banal play imaginable; it is banal only in the sense that its content is trite and tired. In short, we can be assured that a given play is *about* something. Our third question then is: "What is this play about?" This is not the same question as "What does this play mean?" Yes, plays, especially the best of them, are meaningful, but analysis is not about reducing the play to a single sentence stating its meaning. To say, for example, that *Othello* tells us that jealousy can lead to madness does not really say much about the play. Nor would we learn much about *Hedda Gabler* if we were to declare that the play teaches us that boredom can lead to dangerous behavior. Our understanding of *The Three Sisters* is not enhanced by reducing it to the statement, "Dreaming about a goal does not get you any closer to it." None of these remarks is wrong, but none is particularly revealing. Nevertheless, it *is* useful to recognize the nucleus of experience in a play. *Othello* is about the debasing effects of jealousy. That is a controlling factor for the play, the focus that works to unify the play's structure. Recognizing this keeps us mindful of what is at the center of the play and keeps us from going off track in describing the effects that shape the play. Similarly, *Hedda Gabler* is about the propensity to exert power over others that is produced by self-absorption and boredom. And *The Three Sisters* is about the human incapacity to perceive or control time. Seen in these ways, the plays take on coherence and meaning without our losing sight of the fact that they are affective experiences. If we find humor or tragedy or pathos in that experience, it is because we sense a parallel in our own lives.

These then are our three questions: "How is this play different from actuality?"; "Why is it different in this way?"; and "What is this play about?" There is a logic to this sequence, a logic related to the opacity–transparency principle discussed earlier. On our first encounter with a script, we are initially aware of its opacity. It has a title, a restricted cast of characters, a "place" somehow depicted on stage, and a time frame all its own. Next we "move into" the play and experience it empathetically. The effects become clear. Finally, we measure the script against our own experience and, in the spirit of aesthetic distance, sense the play's meaning. In other words, a play refers inwardly to its structure and manipulation of materials and outwardly to engage the audience, and then extends beyond itself to refer to some aspect of human experience. This is what Suzanne Langer meant by her "opacity–transparency" principle.

The Three Readings

Although is not literally true that analysis requires three readings of a script, separating the endeavor in this way clarifies what the process calls for. In any event, there is certainly no harm in doing three readings. Each of the three serves a distinct purpose. If we do conduct the analysis in two readings or even in one reading, we still have to accomplish all the steps described in the following three readings.

The First Reading

The first is the quietest reading. We should do it calmly and relatively quickly, preferably in one sitting. The idea is to allow ourselves simply to experience the play, to let the play happen in its own time. At this stage, we should not question every moment, worry over structure, or seek meanings. Doing the reading in one sitting helps ensure that we are mindful of the play's movement in time and its building of effects. To stop in midstream is to introduce distractions that may require rereading large portions of the script.

At the very start, the title, cast of characters, set description, and opening action contribute to the basis of the entire play to come. It is worthwhile to spend time examining these items closely before moving into the play's scripted action. What do these things tell us about the world of the play? What implications are inherent in the title? Does it provoke associations or suggest tone? The cast of characters likewise may tell us a great deal. Groupings may imply potential tensions. The names or lack of them may matter. Are relationships already apparent in the descriptions of the characters? Are they associated with any particular national, ethnic, or political group? Is the style of the play apparent in the cast list? Next, the set description can be thorough or sketchy, but in either case we gain some appreciation of the appearance of the stage as the curtain or lights go up. Is it highly detailed? Is it relatively bare and suggestive for the imagination? Is it formal and abstract, or messy and realistic? These and other questions may find answers in the set description. Sometimes the script provides a breakdown in terms of time and place of the scenes that will make up the play. And that too needs to be examined. Finally, the very first impression as the action gets under way is almost always telling. A certain tension will already be apparent. The initial positions of the characters and the way they relate to the audience can powerfully suggest the experience we are about to embark on. So savor these initial matters. Let them sink in for a moment. Then proceed with a quick and quiet reading of the script. Pause just a moment at the end of each formal segment to sense the parting effect before starting the next scene or act. There may be a new set description at that moment. Certainly the opening action of the new scene or act gives us a new motif on which to base anticipation of the new tensions.

At the end of the script, reflect on the play as a whole. The concluding action and the last impression are terribly important to the play. What is the final effect? Begin now to make notes about the play. At what point would you locate the crux moment, the climax, when all tension has snapped? Are you quite sure there is no further tension after that moment? If that is the climax, what are the two sides of the tension that snapped? Has it operated throughout the play? If not, you may have mistaken the climax. If so, at what point in the early stage of the play did the driving force emerge to work against resistance? Are the climax moments of the formal segments (acts and scenes) related to the overall tension? Does the play have a protagonist and if so, who is it? What tensions emerge in relation to the context of the play: between the present and the past or between the place of the action and places beyond our view? What is the nature of the audience's involvement? How does the play open to us? What is asked of us in terms of emotional involvement and critical assessment? What is this play about?

The Second Reading

At the end of the first reading, you made only some tentative notes, but you asked questions to which you ultimately need answers. You may not have all the answers and you may not be convinced about some of those you do have. The second reading should clear up some of these ambiguities. The second is the closest reading. This time you know where the action is going, so you can be much more alert to how it gets there. Turning again to the title, the cast of characters, and the set description, what do they suggest about the world of the play, its probability, and set of tensions? The title now may have richer connotations. The characters may now group themselves in a meaningful way. The setting may imply tensions that you now know will be tapped. Moving further into the script, it is useful to make pencil marks at those moments when the tension shifts and realigns itself, the beginnings and ends of organic segments. Major reversals or changes will send the action off in new directions, creating landmark moments and the beginnings of new sequences of action. You might mark these moments with a double slash. Toward the end of each formal segment, look for and mark the climax, the moment when tension snaps. Significant statements, passages, or dramatic effects deserve check marks or underscoring. Stay mindful of the uses being made of scenery, lights, costumes, sounds, properties, and so forth. What is the relationship between the actor and the character he or she portrays? Are we asked to forget that actors are playing these parts? Or are we reminded in some way that the performers before us are not literally the characters? At the end of the second reading, check the notes you have made. How accurate are they now after that thorough reading? What alterations or refinements would you make? Make new and more detailed notes.

The Third Reading

Having studied the script closely in the second reading, you should now be able to read through the script to check your ideas. Look for things this time that might contradict your thinking. Play the devil's advocate with yourself. It is important that you let the play be what it is. Don't try to force it to say what you would like it to say. This last reading is fairly quick, basically a double check, and it works best if done in one sitting, just as you did the first reading. At the end of this third reading, polish and refine your notes. Did questions arise in the reading that call out for explanation? You must now be satisfied that you have grasped how the play works and why it does so. Now, finally—what is this play about?

The Final Analysis

Presenting the analysis is a matter of organizing your notes. You arrived at the notes through an empirical process of gathering the evidence, putting together the details in such a way that they took on coherence. Now you must work backward, stating at the beginning the basic subject and tensions operating in the play, and then supporting this conclusion with details within the play. This provides a structure that will organize your thoughts, whether you are writing about the play, putting together your approach to it as a director, sensing your character's relationship to the play as a whole as an actor, or looking for useful patterns as a designer. The structure might look something like the following:

1. At the outset, isolate what the play is about. What in the nature of human experience is at the center of the play?

2. Follow that up by describing how the play uses its material. Every play exists in a context on both the fictional and the actual levels. You might refer to such things as the way the play defines the stage space, how it opens itself to the audience, how it uses time, and the nature of its fictional world, including its characters.

3. Describing how the play uses its material should lead to isolating the essential tension of the play. What factors are at odds, in conflict, or in contrast to one another? How do the formal segments (acts or scenes) reenforce that tension?

4. This should lead to a discussion of the driving force of the play, the sources of resistance, and the climax.

5. Now look for support for these general patterns. You may find it in how the action is cut off from previous times or how the place is cut off from other places. The way in which segmentation operates ought to illustrate the basic tension. Character groupings and relationships should also yield insights pertinent to the play as a whole. Are there any telling contrasts or conflicts among them? Are there any disparities or ironies between the characters' view of events and the audience's? How does the play enlist the audience's imagination and empathy? Some of these questions will be much more pertinent than others depending on the specific play under examination. Some, may in fact, be irrelevant. Nevertheless, this should be a useful list of places to look for support of your general assessment of the play structure and effects.

6. Take the long view again: What is the play's ultimate effect? When it is over and the curtain has come down, what is the audience members's state of mind? What is their mood? What are they left reflecting on?

Certainly, you need not explore every avenue of expression used in the play. There is no need to explore and describe every organic segment in the play. Nor should your analysis account for every single instance of a contrast, irony, incongruity, conflict, or other tension. The purpose of analysis is to isolate what is most pertinent and meaningful in the experience the play produces. Let that take focus, and the rest should fall into place.

Analysis for Directors and Actors

Directors and actors have a special relationship to a play in the making. They see to the embodiment of the play. The characters will become flesh and blood courtesy of the actors who breathe life into them. Their interactions, under the guidance of the director, should create an ensemble, the illusion of the first time, and the rhythms and tempo of the action. The director, moreover, is charged with establishing a production concept for the play that has its basis in the analysis of the play but also takes into account the specific stage on which the play will be mounted, the audience likely to engage with it, and the outside world, where political issues, social problems, philosophical perspectives, and scientific discoveries can influence the play itself. Most plays have the capacity to echo the outside world in which it is performed. Those that do not are, for all intents and purposes, dead. This factor often leads directors and actors to shift the setting or time of the play's action or to emphasize one quality in the play over another. Doing so can enhance the intensity of the audience's engagement with the play. Some interesting examples come from two productions by the Royal National Theatre, one of J. B. Priestley's *An Inspector Calls* and the other of Shakespeare's *Richard III*. The latter play deals with the vicious and oppressive reign of that British king in the fifteenth century, but the production brought it forward to the time of the rise of fascism, especially in the 1930s and 1940s, with Richard an analog of Franco, Mussolini, and Hitler. The former translated the guilt the inspector brings out in the members of the Burleigh household into a collective, social guilt that ignored the needs of the less fortunate and led to war. In a different case, director Joanne Akalaitis chose to emphasize certain qualities relating to the blight of cities and issues of race in Samuel Beckett's *Endgame* by staging the play in an abandoned subway tunnel and casting a black actor as Hamm.

Some of the alterations made in settings or emphasis can give new life to an old and worn-out play, revitalizing a familiar classic. They can also distort the play, as Beckett seems to have believed when he threatened to bring suit against Akalaitis and the American Repertory Theatre for the changes they made to his play. Worse than that, they can actually cripple the play and render it meaningless. If the production concept is not rooted in close analysis, it can easily go astray.

At the very outset of the production process, the director is alone with the script. There will come a time when many people will be involved in the production process, and the director must be ready to work with them, inspire their artistic efforts, and lead them to the realization of a unified and compelling production. None of that can happen without analysis. The vertical analysis described earlier can be a useful device during this reflective phase. Passing through the three readings, the director can break down the action into meaningful units: organic segments, or beats, or simply French scenes. In any event, each of these units will draw on several different sources: actors' activity, setting and properties, costumes and makeup, and lighting and sound. Each of these has something to contribute to the effect of the segment. One way to keep track of these avenues of expression and how they can contribute is to draw up a table, making a vertical list of the segments of action accompanied by columns, each referring to a different avenue of expression that the theatre affords: scenery, costumes, lights, sound, properties, activity. Working across these columns, we can single out ways in which one or another of these elements supports the effect of the segment. Not all of them will contribute in any significant way, but those that do can be singled out and described here.

The director ought to emerge from this brown study with a firm idea of how the various parts of production can contribute to the overall effect. He or she should be ready to describe what each designer can contribute to the various aspects of production. There is nothing dictatorial about this; it is a matter of communicating. The descriptions will need to be translated into visual terms, and that is the business of designers, not directors. Identifying the materials that spark the imagination of designers to visualize the work is the business of the director. Some directors communicate through metaphors, even selecting a fundamental metaphor that informs the entire production. A metaphor, of course, is a likeness, a parallel between the play's experience and another experience. In the case of Sam Shepard's *Buried Child*, for example, a controlling metaphor might be found in the image of hidden rot and decay. Such an image may find reflection in the design of the play as well as in its action: Dodge's body-wracking cough, stained and torn open shirt, threadbare couch, distressed wallpaper, ragged carpet, and so forth. The more vivid and articulate the director can be in communicating with the designers, the more likely it is they will produce visual and aural effects not only pertinent to the show but also powerful in their support.

Working with the actors is another matter, although it also must have its roots in solid analysis. Directors are often more direct, specific, and detailed in dealing with designers than with actors. Actors must find their own way into the characters they portray. In some spirit, they will live the lives of those characters. That means that the creation of a role requires experiencing it and experimenting with it. The director is obliged to let this happen. Being prescriptive will not help, but he or she can guide the explorations and open up possibilities. If the actors are given the director's analysis and concept in full detail, they will feel they have nothing to contribute of their own and nothing to discover. The director is there to be sure the production concept does not get lost.

This is not to say that the actors will not busy themselves with analysis. On the contrary, they cannot avoid doing analytical work with the script. Some form of analysis goes into every decision an actor makes. Again, the more methodical the analysis process is for the actor, the more efficient and effective it will be. Everything laid down here in the form of steps in analysis applies to actors as well. Beyond that, the actor must apply special study to the character as presented in the script. The following points are useful in this process:

1. What do we know about this character's drive or desire? What does he or she want? What is the overall objective behind the decisions the character makes throughout the play?
2. How and where do the character's motivations shift in the progress of the play's action? These shifts are tied to the beats or organic segments of the play.
3. What is the character willing (and unwilling) to do to achieve her or his objective?

4. What can we glean from the script about what the character looks like?
5. What do we know about what the character did or experienced before the time of the play's action? What effects are evident in the present time?
6. What relationships does the character have with each of the other characters? What do they share in the past? What does the character want out of them, and what do they want out of the character? How do their relationships change?
7. What do we know, if anything, about the character's future beyond the end of the play?
8. Finally, and perhaps most important, how does the character contribute to the play as a whole? Why is the character even in the play?

These questions will have more or less pertinence depending on the specific play. In fact, it can be very revealing to note what kinds of things we do know about a character and what kinds of things we do not know; such revelations expose much about what matters in the play as a whole. We know nothing, for example, about what Oedipus looks like or how he likes his eggs in the morning, but we do know that Stanley Weber (in Pinter's *The Birthday Party*) likes having cornflakes for breakfast and we know that he wears glasses. On the other hand, we eventually learn a great deal about Oedipus's past and very little about Stanley's.

The questions certainly can yield useful insights. Their answers may in fact form the basis for much of the exploration entailed in the rehearsal process, especially in the early phases of the polishing rehearsals. Something out of the past may spark something happening now. Something the character knows about another character could give an edge to a scene they have together. The fact that the character has a hidden affection for one character and harbors a deep-seated resentment against another may help in playing a scene. All of this transpires in the rehearsal process as actors make discoveries and build a sense of ensemble. By the end of the rehearsal process, the play may attain a rich spontaneity that would not have been possible had the director and the actors not started with analysis.

Analysis for Designers

It falls to the designers to provide the world of the play. What that world looks and sounds like is their business. Again, this requires close analysis of the script. Of course, the script gives only some indications about design. As a collection of words in the form of dialogue and stage directions, it has nothing visual to offer. The actors have the advantage of knowing the words they will speak, but the designers may have only a few descriptive directions, and then must glean from hints in the script—hints such as the nature of the action, its style, the apparent mood and atmosphere, character relationships, and so forth—just how the world of the play ought to look (or sound, in the case of the sound designer). Some of the stage directions may include a description of the setting or of the clothes the characters wear, or there may be indications of light changes and sounds. But no matter now detailed they may be, they are simply descriptions. Moreover, they are generalized descriptions written without regard for the particular stage and theatre in which the designers work. They are just words.

The director also provides a concept in the form of written or spoken words. The designers work from words into the senses, particularly the senses of sight and sound. Thus, they seek to translate values inherent in the play into sensory experience. Having to make the translation of the script into visual terms makes analysis that much more important. Designers profit from undertaking the same three readings as the other artists. They will, however, add some special considerations in those readings, especially the third one. They are looking for specific requirements inherent in the script. Designers (scenic, costume, lights, sound) share many of the same concerns, and they work with the same basic principles. In fact, it is not unusual for the same person to undertake the total design. Nevertheless, each category has its own special concerns. For that reason, it would be well to examine the analysis process of each of these designers separately.

The Scenic Designer

The task of the scenic designer is to define and characterize the stage space, which is a complex matter. It means making visible such qualities as style, mood, and atmosphere; time period; and the social context of the play's action. It also means configuring the space so as to provide an efficient and expressive "machine for action," allowing for the movements and blocking arrangements that will suit the play's action. Defining how the stage space relates outward to the audience and inward to the implied "world beyond" is also the scenic designer's responsibility.

Every play takes place in a time and a place, both of which may be more or less specific. Some will be very specific and call for a high degree of detail. Such is the case with virtually any realistic play (such as Ibsen's *A Doll's House* or Wilson's *The Piano Lesson*) and with many that are not technically realistic (such as Pinter's *The Birthday Party* or Shepard's *Buried Child*), as well as with plays set in a particular historic period and locale (such as Miller's *The Crucible* set in Salem, Massachusetts, in the seventeenth century, or Shaffer's *Amadeus* set in Vienna in the eighteenth century). These sorts of plays require the designer to find good examples of the architecture and typical decor employed at the time in which the plays are set. Such details should not be slavishly copied, but they can spark the imagination to conjure up a setting that seems to belong to the times. Some plays are themselves period plays (such as Shakespeare's *Othello* or Sheridan's *The School for Scandal*) and rely on stage conventions belonging to the theatre of their time. In such cases, it is always valuable to know what staging practices were in use then because often that knowledge will clarify how the play should play and with what sort of set. At the opposite extreme are plays that make very little reference to or use of the specifics of time and place. Shakespeare's plays are often set in particular places at particular times, but they do not depend on representing those places. *Henry V*, for example, takes place during the reign of that British king in the fifteenth century and in such places as his royal palace, the streets of London, the French royal palace, and the battlefield at Agincourt. The same might be said for Brecht's plays: *Mother Courage* takes place during the Thirty Years War in the seventeenth century and all over central Europe, but the only physical object that is at all specific is Mother Courage's cart.

Configuring the space as a "machine for action" is an important part of the work of the scenic designer. It means analyzing the script carefully for how the action moves about in the space and from scene to scene. In *Henry V*, for example, the action flows continually, every scene coming directly on the heels of the last. It would be useless to try to represent any of the locales, because they succeed one another at such a pace that the effort would cripple the play. Tony Kushner's *Angels in America* has action in multiple locales, sometimes simultaneously, and the more fully these places are portrayed, the weaker the play becomes. Some plays call for two or more locales to exist on stage, as in the case of the kitchen, master bedroom, boys' bedroom, and the yard in Miller's *Death of a Salesman.* This means that although there is some specificity about the rooms themselves, the overall set must accommodate them all and provide for easy and smooth transitions. Even in the case of a realistic play, the set needs to provide for interesting patterns of movement and for emphasis to be available where needed. Analysis of how the action moves in space is a great help in arriving at a useful and expressive setting.

Defining how the stage space relates outward to the audience and inward to the implied world beyond has much to do with the style of the play. How it involves the audience is a measure of how the world is viewed. At one extreme are those plays that are open to the audience, sometimes to the point of incorporating audience members into the action. This is true of most environmental theatre and of many monologue pieces such as *The Vagina Monologues* or the portrait work of Suzi Lori Parks. The audience becomes a sort of confidant of the main character in Margaret Edson's *Wit*, with the result that the stage house has to be a part of the setting for the play. Other plays are deliberately closed to the audience, which is left to peer into the world of the play. This is the case not only of highly realistic plays but also of such unrealistic pieces as Samuel Beckett's *Footfalls* (in which we can see nothing clearly except the lower part of Amy's body as her feet traverse the nine steps that make up her little illuminated space) or Fornes's *The Conduct of Life* (in which the characters are caught in the little cubicles that make up the stage set). The fact that a play is isolated in space means that offstage becomes an extension of the visible world on stage. The set designer often must take that into account and create a setting that implies what is out there. This may mean creating a believable architecture for the house containing the room we see on stage. The set can even imply vividly where characters come from when they enter and where they go to when they exit.

In short, analysis of the uses of stage space, the alignment of tensions, and the nature of the movement of action from segment to segment and scene to scene is basic to the creative work that the scenic designer undertakes. There is still a wide latitude for creative invention. Moreover, that invention will be all the more effective the more firmly it is based on analysis.

The Costume Designer

Much of what has been said of the scenic designer applies as well to the costume designer. They are both concerned with creating the visible world of the play, so the same design elements and principles apply to both of them. The difference is that the costume designer is designing the people who occupy the world the set designer gives them. "Designing the people" is an exaggeration, of course, because the costume designer designs only what each actor will wear, but some costumers would very much like to design the entire person. But then, just as the set designer must work with the actual stage on which the play is to appear, the costume designer must work with the actors cast. In any event, the task here again is to define and characterize the world of the play: its mood and atmosphere, its time and place, its style, and its social context. This time the task is in the medium of costume.

Costume can tell us a great deal about character and about the play as a whole. Like sets, costumes can tell us about the period and the locale in which the action is set. Eighteenth-century ladies and gentlemen of London dressed very differently from the Veronese of the fifteenth century or the colonists and Indians of seventeenth-century America. We also sense something about the time of year or the time of day from the costumes. Costumes help establish the social standings of characters and they may in some instances, such as through uniforms, indicate occupation. Costume may even reveal something of a character's social attitude, such as snobbish, disaffected, rebellious, or indifferent. It also can aid the actor in portraying the psychological state of the character. A character with a penchant for playfulness and another given to strict and dour seriousness are likely to exhibit these traits in their costumes. Perhaps most valuable is the fact that costumes can help create character relationships through visible cues. A motif appearing in one costume may be subtly repeated in another. The Montagues and the Capulets in *Romeo and Juliet* can be visually differentiated by costume color or patterns.

For costumes to fulfill these functions, a close analysis of the script is necessary. The usual revelations that can come through the three readings of the script are always useful. The costume designer's decisions affect the establishment of the various tensions at work, the characters' backgrounds and relationships, and the mood and atmosphere. This analytical work parallels in some ways what the actors are doing in examining their characters. Both, after all, characterize the characters. The objective of a character, the shifting motivations from scene to scene, and the relationships with others are all relevant. One special matter for the costumer is the pattern of encounters the characters go through: who meets whom when and where? A character distribution chart can be useful for recognizing this because it lays out clearly who is on stage with whom and in what scene. It can also show when in the course of the action a change of costume is required. The stage picture depends on a considered and balanced costume design.

Colors, silhouettes, fabrics, textures, layering, and accessories are all available to express character and the nature of the world of the play. As with set design, the costumes need to reflect the way in which the play opens to its audience and the style of its distinctive world. Costumes are not the same as clothes; they are intended for presentation and effect. And, again, we need to sense the world the audience occupies, for the play, including the costumes, is also a part of that world. What out there are we reflecting in here? That is a question for the entire production team. It may lead the director and the designers to set the play in a time and place other than the one the script calls for. Doing so runs the risk of undoing what is at the core of the play's experience, but if it does not do that, it can enhance effect and lend new meaning to the play.

The Light and Sound Designers

These two are grouped together because their work is tied to time in a way the others' work is not. We sense light and sound as they occur and as they change. Their most expressive qualities lie in their mutable nature. Light is a mysterious substance in that we do not sense it until it reflects off of something. When it does, it can change the appearance of the set and the characters in an instant. A change of angle, a lowering or raising of intensity, or a shifting of color can make a dramatic difference. Sound can come and go. We can hear it as an undercurrent subtly reenforcing a mood, sneaking in and quietly fading away without our noticing. We can hear it as a part of the world of the play: a door slam, a train passing by, and so forth. The manipulation of light and sound can create strong effects that enhance mood, establish emphasis, restrict or redefine acting space, or add new dimensions of stage reality.

The light designer can control a number of variables to gain effect: light intensity, color, angle, distribution, and movement. Studying the script, the light designer can establish, in tandem with the set design, a meaningful distribution of light over the stage in a way that throws emphasis where it belongs in any given scene. Light contributes greatly to the composition of the stage picture at any point in the developing action of the play. The succession of organic segments causes shifts in emphasis and subordination, and in some instances light can support those shifts. Mood and atmosphere can emerge strongly out of careful manipulation of light, especially through uses of angles and colors. Light can also enhance the style of the play. If the play is realistic, the light can suggest time of day or year or create natural room light. If it is a piece of epic theatre, the presence of the lights may be blatant and forceful. If absurdist, it might be slightly askew and strange in its angles. If symbolistic or impressionistic, the light is apt to be muted, drifting, and somewhat hazy. Making these decisions requires a firm grasp of the values inherent in the script.

Sound is of two kinds: live or recorded. It can be related to the fictional world of the play in two different ways: (1) It may be part of the fictional world, or "diagetic," and appear to be sounds coming from what is real to that world, such as a doorbell buzzing, a telephone ringing, a car starting, a wind in the chimney; or (2) sound can be outside the world of the play, or "nondiagetic," and exist as a comment on it or as a support for the mood; such sound is almost always recorded sound and most often music. Some sounds are explicitly called for in the script, perhaps even referred to in the dialogue. The designer does, however, have latitude beyond that to create sounds of both kinds: birds chirping on a spring morning, crickets chirping in a summer evening, or an undercurrent of music. In any case, the sound should be bound up in the nature and effects of the play. Any sound or light that detracts from the play is worse than useless.

Two last things may be said of the work of designers in general. First, their analysis of the script is apt to make greater use of metaphor and imagery than is the case for the director or the actors. Metaphors and images arouse visual associations that can be effective ways of engaging the audience in the spirit of the play. Related to that concern is the recognition that the process of play production is collaborative. The exchange of ideas in early production conferences and all the way through the creative process can always yield fresh approaches to the mutual task. Nevertheless, it rests with the director to make the final decisions. Without that controlling vision, the production could become a pastiche of multiple styles, creating enough confusion to drag the play into artistic incoherence.

A Few Last Words

The approach to script analysis outlined here grows out of a conviction that plays, for which scripts are the essential design, realize their full essence in occupying a stage and confronting an audience. The stage, of course, is not at all the same as the page. Nevertheless, the page contains the indications, implicitly if not explicitly, as to the nature of the play's ultimate stage embodiment. The method described in this chapter is intended to help us be mindful of the stage context called for in the script. We also need to be alert to the way in which effects are shaped in time, as organic segments succeed one another and round out in formal segments. Shifting tensions carry us through the play to its concluding moment. These tensions narrow to a point at which the action snaps, causing a sudden break in tension. That moment, the crux or climax, is a significant and telling moment because it clarifies what was at the heart of the play's action in terms of conflict, contrast, irony, incongruity, or disparity, which in turn informs all of the play's action.

This method can be an aid not only to the reading of a script but also in producing it as a play on stage. Decisions made by the director, the actors, and the designers may be highly creative, even ingenious. If, however, they are not somehow anchored in analysis, they are likely to lead to a show so excessively brilliant as to be meaningless. None of this means there is only one way to produce a particular play, a way spelled out in its script. That would be absurd—as if the only creative artist in the theatre is the playwright and all the others must engage in a guessing game about exactly how the script should be realized. Still, the script is the basis for the production, and those artists producing it need to be sensitive to and aware of what matters in the play once on stage.

The audience is the final and most important factor. The play is intended for human observers, and without them the play is really not a play. The audience will make connections, accept allusions, sense the inner lives of the characters, absorb the visual effects and moods, and finally reflect on the experience. It is in a sense the ultimate collaborator after the playwright, director, actors, and designers. Every one of those creative artists calculates on the basis of audience reception. The audience contributes its own sense of human life and links it with the depiction inherent in the play. Only then does the play assume its fullest measure of meaning. We should be able to describe not only how a play is put together but also how it reflects the human condition. Plays are not self-contained structures; they deliberately open themselves, one way or another, to an audience. They are controlled experiences that, strange to say, the audience helps to control. Scripts could never be turned into plays if that were not the case. Directors, actors, and designers need to be able to make the leap from page to stage. Anyone can make that leap. It requires a disciplined sensitivity and a capacity to make oneself into a hypothetical audience member while reading. "Disciplined sensitivity" is what this book is all about.

APPENDIX A

Sample Analysis
On the Harmfulness of Tobacco
by Anton Chekhov

Following is the full text of a short play by Anton Chekhov that will serve as the basis for a sample analysis. It is an intriguing piece partly because of its curious and paradoxical tone. Although it amuses us, it also strikes us as pitiful. Another source of interest is the double existence the play assigns to the audience and ultimately even to the character. *On the Harmfulness of Tobacco* is a simple play in that it requires nothing much more than an actor wearing a frock coat and standing before an audience, and yet its complexities make it fascinating.

On the Harmfulness of Tobacco

Nyukhin: *(He enters the stage with great dignity, wearing long side whiskers and a worn-out frock coat. He bows majestically to his audience, adjusts his waistcoat, and speaks.)* Ladies and . . . so to speak . . . gentlemen. It was suggested to my wife that I give a public lecture here for charity. Well, if I must, I must. It's all the same to me. I am not a professor and I've never finished the university. And yet, nevertheless, over the past thirty years I have been ruining my health by constant, unceasing examination of matters of a strictly scientific nature. I am a man of intellectual curiosity, and, imagine, at times I write essays on scientific matters—well, not exactly scientific, but, if you will pardon me, approximately scientific. Just the other day I finished a long article entitled: "On the Harmfulness of Certain Insects." My daughters liked it immensely, especially the part about bedbugs. But I just read it over and tore it up. What difference does it make whether such things are written? You still have to have naphtha. We have bedbugs, even in our grand piano. . . . For the subject of my lecture today I have taken, so to speak, the harm done mankind by the use of tobacco. I myself smoke, but my wife told me to lecture on the harmfulness of tobacco, and so what's to be done? Tobacco it is. It's all the same to me; but, ladies and . . . so to speak gentlemen . . . I urge you to take my lecture with all due seriousness, or something awful may happen. If any of you are afraid of a dry, scientific lecture, cannot stomach that sort of thing, you needn't listen. You may leave.

(He again adjusts his waistcoat.)

Are there any doctors present? If so, I insist that you listen very carefully, for my lecture will contain much useful information, since tobacco, besides being harmful, contains certain medicinal properties. For example, if you take a fly and put him in a snuff box, he will die, probably from nervous exhaustion. Tobacco, strictly speaking, is a plant. . . . Yes, I know, when I lecture I blink my right eye. Take no notice. It's simple nervousness. I am a very nervous man, generally speaking. I started blinking years ago, in 1889, to be precise, on September the thirteenth, the very day my wife gave birth to our, so to speak, fourth daughter, Varvara. All my daughters were born on the thirteenth. But . . . *(He looks at his watch.)* time at our disposal is strictly limited. I see I have digressed from the subject.

I must tell you, by the way, that my wife runs a boarding school. Well, not exactly a boarding school, but something in the nature of one. Just between us, my wife likes to complain about hard times, but she has put away a little nest egg . . . some forty or fifty thousand rubles. As for me, I haven't a kopek to my name, not a penny . . . and, well, what's the use of dwelling on that? At the school, it is my lot to look after the housekeeping. I buy supplies, keep an eye on the servants, keep the books, stitch together the exercise books, exterminate bedbugs, take my wife's little dog for walks, catch mice. Last night, it fell to me to give the cook flour and butter for today's breakfast. Well, to make a long story short, today, when the pancakes were ready, my wife came to the kitchen and said that three students would not be eating pancakes, as they had swollen glands. So it seems we had a few too many pancakes. What to do with them? First my wife ordered them stored away, but then she thought awhile, and she said, "You eat those pancakes, you scarecrow." When she's out of humor, that's what she calls me: "scarecrow," or "viper," or "devil." What sort of devil am I? She's always out of humor. I didn't eat those pancakes; I wolfed them down. I'm always hungry. Why yesterday, she gave me no dinner. She says, "What's the use feeding you, you scarecrow. . . ." However . . . *(He looks at his watch.)* I have strayed from my subject. Let us continue. But some of you, I'm sure, would rather hear a romance, or a symphony, some aria . . .

(He sings.)

"We shall not shrink In the heat of battle:
Forward, be strong."

I forget where that comes from. . . . Oh, by the way, I should tell you that at my wife's school, apart from looking after the housekeeping, my duties include teaching mathematics, physics, chemistry, geography, history, solfeggio, literature, and so forth. For dancing, singing, and drawing, my wife charges extra, although the singing and dancing master is yours truly. Our school is located at Dog Alley, number 13. I suppose that's why my life has been so unlucky, living in house number thirteen. All my daughters were born on the thirteenth, I think I told you, and our house has thirteen windows, and, in short, what's the use? Appointments with my wife may be made for any hour, and the school's prospectus may be had for thirty kopeks from the porter.

(He takes a few copies out of his pocket.)

Ah, here you see, I've brought a few with me. Thirty kopeks a copy. Would anyone care for one?

(A pause.)

No one? Well, make it twenty kopeks. *(Another pause.)* What a shame! Yes, house number thirteen. I am a failure. I've grown old and stupid. Here I am, lecturing, and to all appearances enjoying myself, but I tell you I have such an urge to scream at the top of my lungs, to run away to the ends of the earth. . . . There is no one to talk to. I want to weep. What about your daughters, you say, eh? Well, what about them? I try to talk to them, and they only laugh. My wife has seven daughters. Seven. No. Sorry, it's only six. Now, wait, it is seven. Anna, the eldest, is twenty-seven; the youngest is seventeen. Ladies and gentlemen:

(He looks around surreptitiously.)

I am miserable: I have become a fool, a nonentity. But then, all in all, you see before you the happiest of fathers. Why shouldn't I be, and who am I to say that I am not? Oh, if you only knew: I have lived with my wife for thirty-three years, and, I can say they are the best years of my life . . . well, not the best, but approximately the best. They have passed, as it were, in a thrice, and, well, to hell with them.

(Again, he looks around surreptitiously.)

I don't think my wife has arrived yet. She's not here. So, I can say what I like. I am afraid . . . I am terribly afraid when she looks at me. Well, I was talking about my daughters. They don't get married, probably because they're so shy, and also because men can never get near them. My wife doesn't give parties. She never invites anyone to dinner. She's a stingy, shrewish, ill-tempered old biddy, and that's why no one comes to see us, but . . . I can tell you confidentially

(He comes down to the edge of his platform.)

on holidays, my daughters can be seen at the home of their aunt, Natalia Semionovna, the one who has rheumatism and always wears a yellow dress covered with black spots that look like cockroaches. There you can eat. And if my wife happens not to be looking, then you'll see me . . .

(He makes a drinking gesture.)

Oh, you'll see I can get tipsy on just one glass. Then I feel so happy and at the same time so sad, it's unimaginable. I think of my youth, and then somehow, I long to run away, to clear out. Oh, if you only knew how I long to do it! To run away, to be free of everything, to run without ever looking back. . . . Where? Anywhere, so long as it is away from that vile, mean, cheap life that has made me into a fool, a miserable idiot; to run away from that stupid, petty, hot headed, spiteful, nasty old miser, my wife, who has given me thirty-three years of torment; to run away from the music, the kitchen, my wife's bookkeeping ledgers, all those mundane, trivial affairs. . . . To run away and then stop somewhere far, far away on a hill, and stand there like a tree, a pole, a scarecrow, under the great sky and the still, bright moon, and to forget, simply forget. . . . Oh, how I long to forget! How I long to tear off this frock coat, this coat that I wore thirty-three years ago at my wedding, and that I still wear for lectures for charity!

(He tears off his coat.)

Take that: And that:

(Stamping on the coat.)

I am a poor, shabby, tattered wretch, like the back of this waistcoat. *(He turns his back showing his waistcoat.)* I ask for nothing. I am better than that. I was young once; I went to the university, I had dreams, I thought of myself as a man, but now . . . now, I want nothing. Nothing but peace . . . peace.

(He looks offstage. Quickly he picks up his frock coat and puts it on.)

She is there. My wife is there in the wings waiting for me. *(He looks at his watch.)* I see our time is up. If she asks you, please, I beg of you, tell her that her scarecrow of a husband, I mean, the lecturer, myself, behaved with dignity. Oh, she is looking at me.

(He resumes his dignity and raises his voice.)

Given that tobacco contains a terrible poison, which I have had the pleasure of describing to you, smoking should at all costs be avoided, and permit me to add my hope that these observations on the harmfulness of tobacco will have been of some profit to you. And so I conclude. *Dixi et animam levavi!*

(He bows majestically, and exits with grand dignity.)

The End

This is a play about self-loathing. Typical of Chekhov, its tone is mixed; it is simultaneously a comic and a pathetic spectacle. It is most assuredly a spectacle. One man, all alone on stage, makes an embarrassing spectacle of himself. He cuts a ridiculous figure. If this were an actual lecture and we the audience attending it, we would be intensely uncomfortable. Here is a man who has come before us to deliver a learned lecture on the subject of the harmfulness of tobacco, but instead he unburdens himself of all the dissatisfaction he feels with himself. His last line, "*Dixi et animam levavi,*" sums it up: Translated from the Latin, it means "I have spoken and relieved my soul."

On the surface, the action is simple. One man stands at the lecture podium, announces a dry, scientific lecture on the harmfulness of tobacco, then skitters continually off the subject in order to tell his audience his woes—his unhappiness with his wife and his life—then turns and exits to meet his wife and return to the life he abhors. This is the essential action. It gains complexity, however, by the uses Chekhov makes of spatial tension and the roles Nyukhin and the audience play. By manipulating these factors, he opens up Nyukhin's inner life to our view.

Regarding spatial tensions, Nyukhin has come away from Dog Alley, 13, and takes great pleasure initially in simply not being there. He takes some delight in meeting with the audience in the vague and rather absurd hope that we will become his friends, understand him, take pity, and accept him into our hearts. At the same time, he is a nervous wreck, his left eye twitching even as he announces that he is lecturing "and to all appearances enjoying" himself. As the play progresses, we in the audience become less and less friendly. We lose all sympathy for him. We will not even buy the school prospectus at the bargain rate of twenty kopeks. In recognition of this, Nyukhin begins to shift his focus over the heads of the audience to the imagined realm of the pole on the hillside under the moon, a place where he might at last find peace and contentment. He longs to become that pole, or a tree, or a scarecrow, under the great sky, a kind of death-in-life. Spatially, then, the first tension develops between Nyukhin in his domain of the podium and the audience assembled in the lecture hall. This tension is enlarged as he describes his life at the boarding school and the wife he married thirty-three years ago wearing the same frock coat he now wears to give lectures for charity. That offstage space becomes more vivid dramatically when the wife shows up in the wings waiting to take him home. Thus, there are four realms that set up tension in the play: the podium, the hall, Dog Alley, 13, and the hillside. The stage, a simple podium, becomes the meeting ground of lines of tension emanating out of the life Nyukhin lives elsewhere, out of his encounter with the audience, and out of his own subjective mind that transfers him to his hillside. Figure A.1 represents the tensions graphically.

The roles that Chekhov assigns in this play are likewise split or divided. From the very start, we assume a double existence. The audience is both the audience of

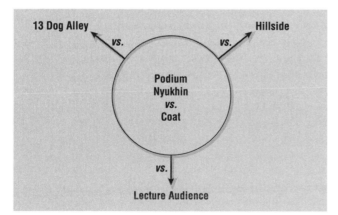

FIGURE A.1 **Diagram representing the four basic spatial tensions in Chekhov's *On the Harmfulness of Tobacco*.**

the play and the audience of the lecture, but the two are not the same. The lecture audience is trapped in an intensely embarrassing situation of watching a man pathetically and absurdly reveal his life and dissatisfactions. The play audience has the advantage of aesthetic distance. Paradoxically, while the lecture audience loses sympathy for the poor man, the play audience experiences a growing empathy for him. Although we laugh at him, for he is outrageously ridiculous, we also glimpse in him a deep-seated agony. Conscious as he is of temporary liberation from his miserable life, he tries very hard to engage us, sometimes by impressing us with his dedication to scientific inquiry and sometimes by sharing his innermost feelings. Nyukhin summons up dignity only to undercut himself. He does so from the beginning, entering grandly and bowing majestically, then announcing, "Ladies and . . . so to speak . . . gentlemen." The undercutting is constant; he breaks even in midsentence. These breaks might be marked by double slashes (//) as follows:

> I am not a professor and I've never finished the university. // And yet, nevertheless, over the past thirty years I have been ruining my health by constant, unceasing examination of matters of a strictly scientific nature. I am a man of intellectual curiosity, and, // imagine //, at times I write essays on scientific matters //—well, not exactly scientific, but, if you will pardon me, approximately scientific. // Just the other day I finished a long article entitled: "On the Harmfulness of Certain Insects." My daughters liked it immensely, especially the part about bedbugs. // But I just read it over and tore it up. What difference does it make whether such things are written? You still have to have naphtha. We have bedbugs, even in our grand piano. . . . // For the subject of my lecture today I have taken, // so to speak, // the harm done mankind by the use of tobacco. // I myself smoke . . .

And so forth. These self-undercuts constitute the organic segments of the play. They also demonstrate the two sides to the lecturer. Like the audience, he too is split into two identities, one of them a dignified scientist and the other a cloying buffoon. The driving force of the play derives from his effort to make peace with himself, first by impressing the audience, then by enlisting the audience as his friend, and finally by projecting himself onto the hillside. Failing on all counts, he attacks himself. He quite literally splits himself in two, taking off his frock coat, throwing it to the ground, and kicking it. These are the major sequences of action. Trampling the coat, he kills himself in effigy, as it were. This is a powerful image of self-loathing.

  That moment is the high point of the play, but it is not the climax. Tension has not yet snapped. He spots his wife offstage. She conveniently had not been there earlier, so he could say what he liked. But now she is there. The climax comes as Nyukhin picks up the coat, puts it back on, and resumes his lecturer persona. We know then that his rebellion has been momentary. He will return to Dog Alley, 13, and to his usual chores, and perhaps he will then await another occasion when he can escape to give still another lecture for charity—although that is not altogether likely, especially if his wife hears how he has behaved. Of course, we won't tell.

APPENDIX B

Sample Analysis
Tartuffe
by Molière

Molière gave *Tartuffe* an alternate title, *The Impostor,* as though he would like us to know that the title character is something of a pretender, a charlatan, a scoundrel. Indeed, the show presents a spectacle of domestic usurpation as Orgon's invited guest, Tartuffe, takes over the house and commands all who reside in it. He *is* an impostor. Posing as a man of devout religion and piety, Tartuffe manages to worm his way into Orgon's confidence. Tartuffe's extraordinary histrionic abilities, playing his pietistic role to everyone in the household, is matched only by the extraordinary gullibility of the master of the house, who believes his presence will serve as a godly model for all his family. The interaction of hypocritical display and gullible acceptance is at the heart of this comic spectacle. Aside from Orgon's mother, Madame Pernelle, no one in the household is taken in by Tartuffe's phony act. Dorine, the maid, takes delight in her verbal undercuts; Elmire, Orgon's wife, maintains her detached dignity; Cléante, the brother-in-law, amazed at what he sees taking place, tries every way he knows to cure Orgon of his obsession; and meanwhile the son, Damis, is outraged (and also disinherited) and the daughter, Mariane, quite simply confused, as is her lover, Valère. No one, not even the audience, is bamboozled here. Nevertheless, the intransigence of the master is powerful enough to frustrate all efforts to disabuse him of his adoration of this charlatan. Therein lies the central tension of the play: the powerful pact between hypocrite and gull set against the effort of the others to undo that power.

Despite the compact and concise structure of the play, very little feeds into it from beyond its boundaries. There is only a brief back story. We learn that Orgon had been impressed with Tartuffe's loud prayers in church, where he found him modestly kneeling beside him and drawing the attention of everyone with his groans and sighs, and that Tartuffe offered the alms Orgon donated to him to other poor people. Out of pity for Tartuffe's impecunious condition and out of admiration for his zealous piety, Orgon has ensconced Tartuffe in his own house, where he hopes Tartuffe's example will be edifying to everyone, including himself. At the outset of the action, Orgon has been away for a few days, and by now Tartuffe has settled in. Later we gain some sketchy information about a casket, which Orgon entrusted to Tartuffe, containing incriminating evidence associated with Argas, a friend of Orgon, who had had to flee the country. We never learn much more about that circumstance. Aside from this background, we hear very little about the world outside this house. Mme. Pernelle makes reference to a neighbor, Orante, whose behavior she regards as modest and exemplary, although only because she has so far passed her prime that she has no choice (according to Dorine).

The action itself is direct and succinct, divided into five formal segments: five acts. Each act has its own distinct function. Each also contains only a few organic segments, but they are all of long duration and usually correspond to the French scenes. Act 1 lays down the circumstances. We learn everything we need to know about the situation through Mme. Pernelle's accusations against the family and her high praise of Tartuffe's piety. The act consists of three organic segments: Madame Pernelle's condemnation of the entire household, Orgon's inquiry into the health of his family and of Tartuffe, and Cléante's first efforts to persuade Orgon to abandon his devotion to this dangerous man. Act 2 concentrates on the forced marriage theme as Orgon insists on his daughter's marrying Tartuffe despite his earlier promise to Valère, which then leads to a lovers' spat that Dorine must help resolve. Act 3 finally introduces Tartuffe himself. The act opens with two brief segments prefacing Elmire's intent to confront Tartuffe; the first segment is between Damis and Dorine as he asserts he will be present at the interview, and in the second Dorine informs Tartuffe that Elmire wishes to speak with him. The main business of the act follows as Tartuffe attempts to seduce Elmire, his host's wife, using flowery sophistry that is interrupted by Damis storming out of the closet. In the final segment, Damis's accusations so outrage Orgon that he throws him out of the house and disinherits him. Act 4 is a little more complicated. It starts with some short segments. First, Cléante attempts to dissuade Tartuffe from continuing his hold over the family. Then Mariane tries to convince Orgon to relinquish his demand that she marry Tartuffe. Elmire's astonishment that Orgon will not believe Tartuffe's lechery leads her to restage the event. Tartuffe is pleased to oblige, but this time Orgon is hidden beneath a table. This at last opens Orgon's eyes. It is too late, however, for act 5 sees Orgon's life falling apart. Tartuffe claims ownership of the house, Valère brings news of Orgon's imminent arrest, and Tartuffe arrives with an arresting officer. The last segment is a marvelous twist: The officer arrests Tartuffe instead on orders from the king. By this point, things have become so desperate that only royal intervention can put things to rights. We learn from the officer that the king has long been aware of Tartuffe's wickedness and only waited this long to see how far the charlatan would go. The king's officer now appears to put things to rights.

This strange and abrupt resolution, funny as it is, has bothered some critics who see it as contrived, a deus ex machina. The plot is constructed with five major reversals. The first, in act 2, is Orgon's decision to force Mariane to marry Tartuffe; the second Tartuffe's attempt at seducing Elmire in act 3, and the third, Orgon's disinheriting and banishing Damis. The fourth is in act 4 when Orgon is finally enlightened upon seeing Tartuffe's second seduction attempt. The final reversal is the royal intercession. The king sends forth his officer to arrest Tartuffe, to restore all of Orgon's property, and to pardon him for any offenses associated with the casket. This is the only reversal that comes from outside the play. There is a good rationale for it to happen, however, and we may find the first clue in examining the conditions surrounding theatrical performances at the time this play was written. These may at first seem extraneous to the script as we have it, but in fact they are built into it in several ingenious ways. We need to bear in mind that the play comes out of an age different from our own and incorporates assumptions we might not readily make.

Background on the Play: Neoclassicism

Tartuffe is a period play from the seventeenth century; the version that has survived dates from 1669. By definition, a period play comes out of another culture that existed in a time and place removed from our own. Inasmuch as scripts are written with the stage in mind, the playwright builds the play on a conception of the available theatre and its audience. Many of the tensions drawn in a play derive in some measure from the conventions the audience of the time would readily accept and from the worldview they would have entertained. These two factors should play into our analysis of *Tartuffe*. Specifically, these factors are how the audience of the mid–seventeenth century saw itself in relation to the stage and how the play taps its perception of reality.

At first this may seem a violation of our own principle of viewing the play on its own terms. To examine the state of mind of audiences of a former time seems not only backward but also impossible. If we are to view a play on its own terms, then we should expect those terms to be built into the play, where we can discover them. This is true. Conventions and a worldview are built into period plays just as they are into contemporary plays. And no doubt with much work we could find them embedded in the script. They were, however, so fully assumed by the dramatist that their presence in the script can be quite subtle. We can save ourselves trouble by becoming knowledgeable about how these two factors apply to the script at hand. Until the late nineteenth century, the acceptance of stage conventions and the sharing of a common view of reality persisted over comparatively long spans of time, enabling us to talk meaningfully about plays of the medieval age, or those of the Elizabethan era, or of the Restoration, or of neoclassical France.

The perspective on reality is, of course, the determining factor in style, as became clear in the previous discussion of form and style. In this case, we are dealing with neoclassicism. With the establishment of the French Academy in 1635, neoclassicism became perhaps the most carefully and rationally codified style in history. It is based on the conviction that truth derives from the close exercise of reason. Nothing is true until it has been distilled to its essence through the operation of the mind. Idiosyncrasies, abnormalities, and anomalies are all irrelevant. What matters most is the universal. Any art form, plays included, must deal with what is *essentially* true. This is a basic principle undergirding all others: the principle of **verisimilitude.** Literally, the term means "likeness to truth" (*veri* = truth; *similitude* = likeness.) According to this principle, plays, as well as other works of art, must bear likeness to truth. In and of itself, this is not an unusual expectation. Most of us expect plays to reflect truth in some way. What makes this distinctive is the neoclassicists' concept of truth as residing in the essence of experience. We can find instances of this in many different art forms of the time. The formal garden, for example, such as the beautifully laid out grounds of the Versailles palace, reflect the essence of "gardenness," where the individual plants and bushes are carefully arranged in beautiful patterns and trimmed to express essential "plantness" and "bushness." Nature left to herself leads to ill-shaped ugliness, according to neoclassicism. Seeds drop willy-nilly here and there, and branches stick out irregularly. They must be manipulated into pleasing and rational shapes. Mountains, unfortunately, must be left to themselves. There was in those days a considerable traffic between France and Italy, necessitating travel through the Alps. These outcroppings were regarded as unseemly and grotesque monstrosities. As it was impossible to trim the mountains into essential "mountainness," the only solution was to pull down the shades on the carriages or avert one's eyes from the horrible spectacle. Not until the romantic era, more than a century later, did people begin to create "natural" gardens and to admire the grandeur of huge craggy mountains.

As with landscaping, playwriting must resort to the essential. It must show us human experience in its very essence. Verisimilitude in the drama was supported by five fundamental principles: decorum; the "utile/dulce" principle; purity of genre; poetic justice; and the three unities. Plays themselves must adhere to their essence as plays: They too should reflect basic "playness." These supporting rules were intended to ensure both that the plays represented the essence of human experience and that they possessed their own essence as plays.

Decorum called for the characters to embody the essence of their age, gender, and station in life. Kings should be "kingly," soldiers "soldierly," young people "youthful," women "womanly," and so forth. The **utile/dulce** (or useful/sweet) principle saw drama as carrying out the double function of being entertaining while also being informative and instructive. Plays should teach and please. **Purity of genre** restricted the number of legitimate dramatic forms to two: tragedy and comedy. Each should adhere to a set of particular characteristics. If a comedy, the play should deal with ordinary people, somewhat worse than average, engaged in everyday, domestic affairs, employing everyday speech, and it should instruct by demonstrating the absurd results of ludicrous behavior and yet always end happily. A tragedy, by contrast, deals with people of high station engaged in affairs of state and speaking an eloquent, elevated language, while the action serves to demonstrate the disastrous results of errors of judgment, and so such plays always end unhappily. Plays that fall outside these characteristics were viewed as irregular. **Poetic justice** derived from the conviction that because plays reflect reality, they also are bound to reflect the work of providence: Ultimately, all is for the best under the rule of a benevolent God. The **three unities** of time, place, and action were conceived to maintain a close concentrated focus for the dramatic action. Unity of action meant quite simply that the plot should be direct, compressed, and well controlled. Subplots or a double plot would detract from and splinter focus.

Time and space posed more complex issues. There had been considerable debate about just how much time should elapse in the fictional world of the play and how wide a space might be represented. Ideally, the time and place ought to correspond to actual time and space: If the action lasts two hours on stage, the same amount of time should elapse among the characters and always in the same place. After all, we in the audience have not moved in the time we spent in the theatre. Neverthe-less, the theorists of the day recognized that some latitude ought to be allowed. As the French Academy finally codified the rules, they stated that the action repre-sented must not extend beyond the duration of a single day and must confine itself to the same general locale from beginning to end. For example, "in and around the castle from early morning to sunset" would be perfectly acceptable, but not "a street in Venice, the Senate in Venice, the ramparts on Cyprus, the streets of Cyprus, a bedchamber on Cyprus, over a few weeks."

At first glance, these rules seem so restrictive as to make writing plays virtu-ally impossible. But they do allow a latitude that might not be immediately appar-ent. In fact, they pose a challenge that could spark creativity. Pierre Corneille, who had his difficulties with the French Academy for having compressed the extensive action of his play *Le Cid* into an unbelievable twenty-four hours, responded with an ingenious solution. He argued that time and space should be treated in such general terms that we are not aware of how much time has passed or how much space has been traversed. If the playwright does not say exactly what time it is, the audience will never know how much later it becomes. By the same token, if the audience does not know precisely where the action is situated, it will never know how far the characters travel. In Corneille's later plays, and in those of Molière and Racine, time and space usually are very generalized. In the case of *Tartuffe*, we are simply in some unspecified room in Orgon's house and apparently in the same day. This is in perfect keeping with the cause of verisimilitude, distilling all experience to its essence. As for decorum, the rule might be adjusted somewhat in the interests of the teaching function of drama. In tragedy, a king behaving indecorously—that is, in an unkingly manner without the wise concern for his people that should inform kingly behavior—could produce great and tragic suf-fering and so demonstrate the need for truly decorous behavior. In a comedy, we can learn a more reasoned behavior by seeing the absurdities that result from excessive indulgence in human weakness. Again, we can have characters violat-ing decorum. Tartuffe, for example, makes himself into a pious, strict, religious man, concealing his indecorous indulgence in gluttony and lechery. The play deliberately exposes his hypocrisy. As Molière declares in his preface to the 1669 version of his play:

> If the purpose of comedy be to chastise human weakness, I see no reason why any class of people should be exempt. This particular failing [religious hypocrisy] is one of the most damaging of all in its public consequences and we have seen that the theatre is a great medium of correction. . . . People can put up with rebukes but they cannot bear being laughed at: they are prepared to be wicked but they dislike appearing ridiculous.

First written in 1664, Molière's *Tartuffe* kicked up such controversy that King Louis XIV banned its performance. The play was without doubt an attack on a particular missionary group operating in France at the time, the Company of the Holy Sacrament. They are never mentioned specifically in the interests of "generalized truth," but they immediately recognized themselves in the play. They happen to have been a powerful group. The Company of the Holy Sacrament dedicated themselves to saving souls by any means, including spying on fellow citizens and publicly exposing their sinful behavior, certain that such exposure would induce repentance. They created an atmosphere of stifling fear as they became more powerful. Molière bound up all the self-righteous hypocrisy of this group into one character, Tartuffe, and demonstrated their capacity to take on an unhealthy control of the French nation through Tartuffe's takeover of the house of Orgon. The company was powerful enough to suppress the play in 1664 and again in 1667 when Molière offered a revised version. He offered still another version in 1669, and this time the king saw fit to allow it. On each of the previous occasions, Molière offered a petition to the king requesting permission to perform the play. The first petition argued that people have played on the king's deep respect for sacred things and that these people, "the Tartuffes," as he calls them, "contrived to find favor with Your Majesty" and managed to have the play suppressed. All this, he says, despite the king's statement that he himself found nothing objectionable in the play. The king had, after all, enjoyed the play from the outset. Much the same sequence of events followed the second version of the play offered in 1667, when Molière declared in his petition that it was useless for him to continue to write for the theatre if the Tartuffes were "to gain the day." But again the play was forbidden. We do not have either of the earlier versions of the play, but the preface to the last version makes clear that one change Molière made was to delay the entrance of Tartuffe until act 3 in order to portray him more fully as a hypocritical scoundrel through the accumulated accounts of him that we hear from his promoters and detractors alike. Readers of the script should note that Tartuffe would not be dangerous at all were it not for the gullibility of the master of the house, Orgon. It is he who brings Tartuffe into the house and he who grants him greater and greater control over all its members.

The House-within-a-House:
Theatrical Conventions

Clearly, *Tartuffe* is a comic spectacle of the dangerous interaction of hypocrisy and gullibility. If the play has endured so well this many years after the demise of the Company of the Holy Sacrament, it is because every society harbors self-righteous organizations or people intent on saving its citizens from some form of perceived evil. They are not dangerous unless we allow them to take control of "our house." Hitler gained power when Germany allowed him to "provide protection" from Jews and other non-Aryans. McCarthy gained tremendous power by promising to save the United States from communists and by stirring up and playing on paranoia. The generalized essence of Tartuffe's takeover of the house of Orgon lends the play continued relevance well after its intended target has vanished. It no doubt will continue to do so.

The theme of *Tartuffe* is supported in interesting ways by the play's engagement with the accepted conventions of the theatre of its day. The fact that we tend to call the auditorium of a theatre a "house" has particular relevance here. The play works as a "house-within-a-house-within-a-house." Like a Chinese box, Orgon's house sits inside the theatre house, which sits inside the house of society at large. The play depends heavily on the interaction between all three of these contexts.

The theatre of Molière's time was constructed in a *box-pit-and-gallery* configuration, which provided an exchange of effects operating on three planes. First of all, the action itself would transpire on the forestage, a level platform area extending out of the proscenium, which itself would have had permanent doors for entrances and exits. This performance space sat between the background scenery and the house and consisted of a series of painted *wings and drops*. A slightly raked stage rose upstage of the proscenium, meeting the vertical wings that tapered at their top with horizontal drops to create a sense of depth to a room or other scenic place. Thus, the action stood out in front of the scenery rather than within it. Unlike realistic staging in which characters occupy their environment and we watch them through an invisible fourth wall, here the actors confront us in our house space as the fictional world stands away and upstage of the actors. Some audience members even paid a little extra to sit onstage with the actors. Meanwhile, out in the house, the audience assembled in three or more tiers of private boxes topped by an open gallery and completely surrounding an open pit, or parterre. The arrangement made audience members very aware of one another. They were encountering not only the actors on stage but also the people assembled in the boxes across the pit or those down in the pit. It is worth bearing in mind that these theatres were illuminated by candlelight from a large chandelier in the center of the ceiling and from sconces along the sides of the house. Naturally, the candles remained lit throughout the show, making everyone fully visible whether onstage or out in the house. We might have seen a number of Tartuffes in that way, one onstage and others in the boxes. Many theatres also had an ornate box at the back of the house called the royal box, which served as the place for the king, other royalty, or nobility to sit and see the show and be seen.

Such a configuration helps account for conventions so liberally used in a play such as *Tartuffe*. It makes asides, for example, very natural in the performance of the play. Because the audience is literally right there, a character can readily break from the other characters to share a private thought with the audience unheard by the others. Dorine does that frequently. Probably one of the best examples, and certainly one of the most telling moments in the play, occurs just as Tartuffe enters in act 3. Just in case anyone might still be entertaining respect for Tartuffe as a holy man, his entrance, Dorine's aside, and his reaction should disabuse that person:

> TARTUFFE: *(Entering and seeing Dorine.)* Laurent, put away my hairshirt and my scourge and continue to pray heaven to send you grace. If anyone asks for me, I'll be with the prisoners distributing alms.

DORINE: *(Aside.)* The impudent hypocrite!

TARTUFFE: What do you want?

DORINE: I'm to tell you . . .

TARTUFFE: For Heaven's sake! Before you speak, I pray you take this hand-kerchief. *(He takes a handkerchief from his pocket.)*

DORINE: Whatever do you mean?

TARTUFFE: Cover your bosom. I can't bear to see it. Such pernicious sights give rise to sinful thoughts.

DORINE: You're mighty susceptible to temptation then! The flesh must make a great impression on you! I really don't know why you should get so excited. I can't say that I'm so easily roused. I could see you naked from head to foot and your whole carcass wouldn't tempt me in the least.

Whereas Dorine is pleased to share her common sense with us in the audience, Tartuffe seems oblivious to our presence. He has no asides to us. Ironically, he is always aware of performing for others but only those in Orgon's house. Ultimately this is his undoing, for he has been watched throughout by the king in his box, and when he has so far overstepped his bounds as to try the royal patience, the king sends his officer onstage to arrest him.

A second convention, one that is richly used in this play, is the graphic picture making the open stage affords. The effect is very like a cartoon. A character may be caught between two others and have to deal differently with each one. A character may be intent on leaving the stage only to be pulled back on. (This occurs in the lovers' spat scene quoted in Chapter 4, pp. 68–70.) Or a character may be hiding under a table while a seduction takes place on the tabletop. Tartuffe's action of extending his handkerchief across the stage to Dorine is a modest example. Because of Orgon's absurd tunnel vision, unable to perceive anything but what is front of him, he provides many examples. In act 2, he confronts Mariane with the demand that she marry Tartuffe rather than Valère, with whom she is in love. Dorine stands behind Orgon's back as he issues orders to his daughter. Dorine's position and her interruptions force Orgon to turn his head to deal with the maid before he can complete his arguments to Mariane, who, being coy and obedient, says nothing. At this point, Dorine has already begun to irritate him with her interruptions:

ORGON: Will you be quiet, you reptile, with your impudent . . .

DORINE: Ah! Fancy a godly man like you getting angry!

ORGON: Yes! This ridiculous nonsense is more than my temper can stand. I insist on your holding your tongue.

DORINE: Right, but I shan't *think* any the less because I don't say anything.

ORGON: Think if you like but take care you don't talk or . . . that's enough. *(Turning to Mariane.)* I've weighed everything carefully as a wise man should . . .

DORINE: It's maddening not to be able to speak. *(She stops as he turns his head.)*

ORGON: Without his being exactly a beauty Tartuffe's looks are . . .

DORINE: Yes! A lovely mug hasn't he?

ORGON: Such . . . that even if his other advantages don't appeal to you . . .

(Orgon turns and faces Dorine, looking at her with arms folded.)

DORINE: She *would* be well off wouldn't she? If *I* were in her place no man would marry me against my will—not with impunity. *I* would show him, ay, and soon after the ceremony too, that a woman has always ways and means of getting her own back.

ORGON: So, what I say hasn't any effect on you at all?

DORINE: What are you grumbling about? I'm not talking to you.

ORGON: Then what *are* you doing?

DORINE: I'm talking to myself.

ORGON: Very well. *(Aside)* I shall have to give her a backhander for her impudence yet.

(He stands ready to box her ears. Dorine, every time he looks at her, stands rigid and without speaking.)

You can't do otherwise, my girl, than approve what I have in mind for you . . . and believe that the husband . . . I have chosen for you . . . *(To Dorine.)* Why aren't you talking to yourself now?

DORINE: I have nothing to say to myself.

ORGON: Not a word even?

DORINE: Not a word, thank you!

ORGON: I was waiting for you . . .

DORINE: I'm not so silly as that!

ORGON: Well, now, my girl, you must show how obedient you are and fall in with my choice.

DORINE: *(Running away.)* I'd scorn to take such a husband! *(He takes a slap at her and misses.)*

We can find many other examples of this graphic picture-making convention. The play in fact opens with one as Madame Pernelle marches across stage in high dudgeon, followed by the bouncing Flipote and the whole of Orgon's household (minus Orgon himself). The lovers' spat in act 2 requires Dorine to keep pulling first one lover and then the other out of the wings to force them to confront each other (see Chapter 4, pp. 68–70). At the end of act 3, Orgon berates his son, Damis, who is standing on one side of him while Tartuffe kneels on the other side pleading for Damis. Then there is the famous image in act 4 of Tartuffe attempting to seduce Elmire on the tabletop while her husband hides beneath the table. Still another instance is the picture in act 5 of Monsieur Loyal ever so politely serving a writ on Orgon ordering him to quit the house, bag and baggage, to make room for Tartuffe, the new owner. All of these images and many more like them provide visual representations of the absurdities produced by the interaction of gullibility and hypocrisy.

Hypocrisy and Gullibility in Collusion

Orgon's side of the equation comes with his astonishing, unquestioning acceptance of the holy righteousness of his new friend, Tartuffe. Were it not for this gullibility, Tartuffe would have no power. But with Orgon's collaboration, Tartuffe claims food and money, Mariane's hand in marriage, an attempt at the seduction of Elmire, the disinheritance of Damis, and finally the house itself, as well as incriminating evidence that could land Orgon in jail. Indeed, Orgon functions as protagonist, not Tartuffe. It is Orgon who brings Tartuffe into the house after hearing his loud prayers at church; it is Orgon who bestows his daughter Mariane on Tartuffe; it is Orgon who deeds his house over to Tartuffe; and finally it is Orgon who entrusts Tartuffe with personal documents that Tartuffe then uses to incriminate him. Tartuffe has merely to take advantage of Orgon's blind devotion. Our first glimpse of this devotion comes in another picture-making scene with Orgon's first appearance on stage. Orgon has returned home after an out-of-town trip and questions Dorine on the state of affairs in the house:

> ORGON: Has everything gone well the few days I've been away? What have you been doing? How is everyone?
>
> DORINE: The day before yesterday the mistress was feverish all day. She had a dreadful headache.
>
> ORGON: And Tartuffe?
>
> DORINE: Tartuffe? He's very well: hale and hearty; in the pink.
>
> ORGON: Poor fellow!
>
> DORINE: In the evening she felt faint and couldn't touch anything, her headache was so bad.
>
> ORGON: And Tartuffe?
>
> DORINE: He supped with her. She ate nothing but he very devoutly devoured a couple of partridges and half a hashed leg of mutton.
>
> ORGON: Poor fellow!
>
> DORINE: She never closed her eyes all through the night. She was too feverish to sleep and we had to sit up with her until morning.
>
> ORGON: And Tartuffe?
>
> DORINE: Feeling pleasantly drowsy, he went straight to his room, jumped into a nice warm bed, and slept like a top until morning.

ORGON: Poor fellow!

DORINE: Eventually she yielded to our persuasions, allowed herself to be bled, and soon felt much relieved.

ORGON: And Tartuffe?

DORINE: He dutifully kept up his spirits, and took three or four good swigs of wine at breakfast to fortify himself against the worst that might happen and to make up for the blood the mistress had lost.

ORGON: Poor fellow!

DORINE: They are both well again now so I'll go ahead and tell the mistress how glad you are that she's better.

Any doubts we might have about whether Orgon has been taken in by this impostor are dispersed by the end of this interview. Again, this is graphic picture making. It is also comical because of the mechanical, unthinking nature of Orgon's responses. Orgon's obsession with piety has rendered him not only comical but also inhumane. Shortly after the interview, he tells Cléante, his brother-in-law, how he had become another man under Tartuffe's influence: "He's teaching me how to forgo affection and free myself from all human ties. I could see brother, children, mother, wife, all perish without caring that much!"

This dangerous combination of hypocrisy and gullibility must meet some sort of opposition to create the driving action of the play. The lineup of characters is such that the extreme of self-righteous, smug hypocrisy represented by both Tartuffe and Monsieur Loyal is set off by the opposite extreme of unthinking, gullible acceptance represented by Orgon and Madame Pernelle. Meanwhile, Damis, Mariane, and Valère are characters so caught up in themselves that they are rendered helpless to effect any change. Three characters, however, represent a balanced view of things, though for contrasting reasons. Dorine does so as a common-sensical wench who impertinently points out the foibles of her master and the lovers. Elmire does so as a dignified, self-possessed, and sane woman who sees things clearly and knows her own mind. Cléante does so as an astonished observer of the excesses going on in this house. He is the voice of reason and stands as the play's *raisonneur*, or spokesman for a rational and balanced view of human conduct. The only thing unreasonable about Cléante is his conviction that if he were to reason with Orgon long enough he could divert him from his foolish convictions. Cléante is absurdly voluble and never recognizes that he is getting nowhere. Everything he says is sound, but his insistence on saying it all is itself almost an obsession. On the other hand, he is in a sense the audience's counterpart on stage: It is as though he had entered Orgon's house by the stage door while we came through the theatre lobby, and both audience and Cléante find themselves fascinated with the spectacle of hypocrisy in league with gullibility.

The arc of action derives from the drive to unmask the charlatan. It requires all the rational persuasion that Cléante, Dorine, and Elmire can put together, the outrage of Damis, the exposure of Tartuffe's lechery for Elmire, and finally the evidence of his perfidy revealed by Monsieur Loyal. As we have seen, the action moves forward in a concise and direct series of scenes that finally culminate in the officer's arrest of Tartuffe. What is peculiar to this play is that it co-opts the audience into the driving force. Orgon may technically be the protagonist, but everything he does provokes a comic outrage in the audience that finally culminates in our sending, with the king's assistance, an officer to put things straight. Dorine enlists our support with her commonsense asides, Cléante expresses our rational convictions, and Elmire conducts the ultimate experiment to expose the scoundrel, but although Orgon is finally persuaded, too much harm has been done and the comedy threatens to end tragically. While Orgon tries to make Madame Pernelle understand the extent of Tartuffe's hypocrisy, experiencing the same frustration everyone felt in trying to convince him, his whole life begins to fall down around him. Monsieur Loyal arrives with his eviction notice, then Valère comes with news of Orgon's imminent arrest, and finally Tartuffe appears bringing the officer whom he expects to carry out the arrest. Orgon's too credulous veneration of this outrageous scoundrel has led not only to his dispossession of the house but also to his personal downfall. It is now too late—except that the king has been watching. The officer arrests Tartuffe instead. This character, who appears at the very end of the play, has only two speeches, the second of which is a long and wonderfully overstated exaltation of the glorious omniscience of the king:

> OFFICER: We live under the rule of a prince inimical to fraud, a monarch who can read men's hearts, whom no impostor's art deceives. The keen discernment of that lofty mind at all times sees things in their true perspective; nothing can disturb the firm constancy of his judgement nor lead him into error.

The officer continues informing us all that the king has long been aware of the baseness of this villain, Tartuffe, and has waited this long only to see how far he would carry his wickedness. That seen, he now puts a stop to it: Tartuffe is arrested, the house and all the goods Orgon had deeded to him are restored, and Orgon is pardoned for the offense Tartuffe had reported in recognition of his past loyalty to the crown.

This strange resolution, funny as it is, is indeed a sort of deus ex machina. And yet it truly grows from the audience's involvement throughout, as though, out of sheer exasperation with Orgon, we must finally step in and put things to rights. And if we cannot do that directly, we can take satisfaction in the fact that we have someone looking after this business who will act on our behalf: the king himself.

Returning to the image of the house-within-a-house-within-a-house, the audience's involvement in pushing for an awakening before all is lost serves as a parallel to the dangers of a takeover of our own society by any of the many self-righteous and self-serving groups or individuals lurking out there. The house of Orgon, set inside the theatre house in its time, became a powerful, even if comic, counterpart to the House of France so threatened by the Company of the Holy Sacrament. The fact that Louis XIV allowed himself to be persuaded to forbid the play, and to do so twice, may well have been the inspiration for incorporating the royal intercession into the resolution of the play. The moment is a wonderfully backhanded compliment to the king. It is also a warning of the danger that exists out there in any society where a king might not intervene.

None of this should be taken to mean that the script is essentially a historical document. It is much more than testimony to the state of affairs in the French nation of the 1660s. We all live in a "house" vulnerable to takeover by charlatans of one stripe or another. Any time it finds its way onto stage, *Tartuffe* has a way of resonating with the outside world. Nor should we feel that the play requires a wing-and-drop, box-pit-and-gallery theatre illuminated by candlelight in order to work. There are many ways to involve the audience in the dynamic of the play without duplicating the original theatrical conditions. But it remains important to find the means. Any production that tries to encapsulate the action inside the stage world will result in a flat and empty experience. The audience is too much a part of the play's dynamic to be left out.

Sample Analysis

The Conduct of Life

by Maria Irene Fornes

First performed in 1985, Maria Irene Fornes's play *The Conduct of Life* belongs to our own time. As such it is constructed assuming an audience much like ourselves. We need not concern ourselves, as we did with *Tartuffe*, with questions of conventions or worldviews distinct from our own. Nevertheless, Fornes sets up her own conventions for the play and infuses it with an intense vision that is at once powerful and ambiguous. People argue over whether to experience the play as a feminist document, and if so, in what sense. Fornes herself has denied that it is. Some of the ambiguity is produced by the strangely abrupt ending. A woman who has been ignored and then abused by her macho, oppressive, vicious husband shoots him dead and turns the gun over to his much abused sex slave and says simply, "Please . . . " and the stage lights fade. On the surface, this would appear to be a vengeful act, not only against the man, Orlando, but also against men in general. Much depends on how we choose to interpret "Please." What Leticia means by that request is left for us to figure out. She may intend for the very young Nena to have the gun so that she can shoot anyone who abuses her in the future. Or she could mean for Nena to take responsibility for the murder, which surely would not be in the spirit of sisterhood. Or she might be asking Nena to use the gun and kill her. We also need to take into account the lost soul that Orlando becomes in the course of the play. Indeed, all the characters, male and female alike, are lost souls caught up in their own emotional cubicles and scarcely able to see much beyond those stifling confines. The politics of the world outside in that unspecified Latin American country contributes powerfully to the deteriorating state of affairs among the characters. A close examination of the episodic organization of scenes (nineteen of them) and the uses of stage space ought to help clarify these issues.

The title of the play, *The Conduct of Life**, is close to something Nena says. In one of the few quiet, sustained scenes (scene 15), she tells the house servant, Olimpia, the story of her miserable life up to that moment, a life of caring for her

*Source: The Conduct of Life in Maria Irene Fornes: Plays. © Copyright 1978 by Maria Irene Fornes. Reprinted by permission of PAJ Publications.

destitute grandfather, living with him in a box on the street, losing track of him, and being taken into a warehouse by Orlando and forced into the role of sex slave. She ends her account in this way:

> He puts his fingers in my parts and he keeps reciting. Then he turns me on my stomach and puts himself inside me. And he says I belong to him. *(There is a pause.)* I want to conduct each day of my life in the best possible way. I should value the things I have. And I should value all those who are near me. And I should value the kindness that others bestow on me. And if someone should treat me unkindly, I should not blind myself with rage, but I should see them and receive them, since maybe they are in worse pain than me.

This is surely not in the same vengeful spirit that some viewers ascribe to the ending of the play. Nena might be the only character to refer to conducting life, but the play as a whole demonstrates several conducts of life that destroy, stymie, or stifle genuine humanity. And they belong to all five of the characters. Ultimately, the play deals with forced and unquestioned roles. These roles are dictated by society and most have some gender basis, but the sad part is that they are also accepted without question. In scene 6, Leticia makes the one statement in the play that comes close to expressing a reaction against these forced roles. When she learns the country's leader has been assassinated and will probably be replaced by someone just as bad, she says:

> We're blind. We can't see beyond an arm's reach. We don't believe our life will last beyond the day. We only know what we have in our hand to put in our mouth, to put in our stomach, and to put in our pocket. We take care of our pocket but not of our country. We take care of our stomachs but not of our hunger. We are primitive. We don't believe in the future. Each night when the sun goes down we think that's the end of life—so we have one last fling. We don't think we have a future.

Several factors contribute to this sense of useless and stifling conduct of life. One is the context in which the play is set, in both its fictional world and its relation to the audience. A second factor is the curious arrangement of pockets of action physically set off from one another in the set. Another is the kaleidoscopic structure of multiple scenes that flash before us, several of them calling for the comings and goings of characters. Finally there is the set of relationships depicted, especially the gradual dehumanizing descent of Orlando.

Regarding the context, many references are made to things beyond the house of Orlando and Leticia. Some of this has to do with the back story, although we know relatively little of the life that has led up to the present state of affairs. We know that Leticia is ten years Orlando's senior and that she "practically brought him up." She was the first woman he loved and she thought he once loved her, but not so now: "I have to look after him," she says, "make sure he doesn't get into trouble. He's not wise. He's trusting." Quite a lot happens in between scenes. At the outset, Orlando is a lieutenant, and by scene 2 he has been promoted to lieutenant commander. Leading into scene 3, Orlando has found Nena on the street, and we see him bring her into the warehouse where he will keep her. Sometime before scene 6 there has been a coup and the assassination of the country's leader, and Orlando has been moved into a new department where he is engaged as an interrogator and torturer—and in fact has already killed a man named Felo. In that scene and in scenes 12 and 16, Leticia talks with a friend named Mona, who seems to be the only person with whom she has a genuine relationship—if Mona exists at all. The political world outside is vicious and corrupt, capable of co-opting people and incorporating them into its machinery. In scene 9, Leticia packs her bag and goes on a trip, leaving Orlando to bring his sex slave into the house. By the next scene, he is in deep trouble over his brutal killing of yet another man. Before scene 14, Leticia has discovered Nena's presence in the cellar, and by scene 15, Nena has become a servant in the house. Sometime between scenes 17 and 18, Orlando has caught wind of Leticia's having a lover. He has confirmation of it at the end of scene 18. This sets up the ugly confrontation in scene 19, the last scene. In short, much activity goes on "out there" and between times.

Meanwhile, the play remains relatively closed to the audience. There are no references to us, no acknowldgement of our presence. These characters live in a strangely trapped domain. Although it is true that they do come and go from the house (all except Nena), no one really leaves: They are always returning to this place. This feeling of entrapment and isolation is reinforced by the pockets created in the setting described in the opening stage directions. Five places are represented on stage, each extending all the way across the stage. Each is at a different level from the others and they are lined up one behind the other. Closest to us is the living room at the level of the stage floor; next is the dining room, eighteen inches higher than the living room; eighteen inches higher than that is a hallway with a door at each end; three feet below that and further upstage is the cellar; and, finally, furthest removed and ten feet high, is the warehouse. Although steps connect each of these levels (except the warehouse), the distinct spaces have the effect of isolating the characters and creating pockets of action.

This sense of isolation, of characters somehow removed from one another, also gains expression in the succession of scenes that flash before us. There is a story here, but the play is not really so much about telling a story. Orlando rises in military rank; kidnaps, rapes, and keeps a young girl; takes a new position as interrogator; kills people; finds out his wife has a lover; and abuses his wife, who then kills him. That is the story. We experience it elliptically and obliquely through scenes that frequently consist of a brief flashing image. The consequent effect produces the feeling of characters caught up in the swirling eddies of the political world unable to see or do anything outside their immediate circumstance.

In the midst of all this, the characters are all in some measure out of touch with one another and even with themselves. The play is peopled by five characters. Three are women occupying roles traditionally dictated as female roles: Leticia, the wife; Olimpia, the housekeeper; and Nena, the child sex slave. Leticia's role as wife has become empty as she becomes progressively estranged from her husband, Orlando. She has no function in life but wishes that she could be educated, perhaps in political science at the university, but she never finished grammar school and must learn to read. She is alienated too from Olimpia, who is determined to run the house her way. Leticia's only contact appears to be the invisible Mona with whom she talks on the telephone. In the first of these phone conversations (scene 6), she tells Mona how concerned she is about the change that has come over Orlando in his new department, and she arranges to go with Mona to a meeting after Orlando has had his smoke. Strangely enough, the second phone conversation with Mona (scene 12) is conducted only in Leticia's mind: She is not actually talking to her. The third conversation (scene 16) again deals with the awful changes that have come over Orlando.

Olimpia too is isolated, partly because of her defective speech and partly because of her obsession with household routines. She has no respect for Leticia and in fact abuses her. She despises Orlando and assaults him, punching him, strangling him, and threatening to cut off his "peepee." Nena, of course, is alienated and dehumanized by having been turned into a sex slave. The two men are in sharp contrast to each another but in both cases lack any capacity to relate to others. Orlando tries to deny himself sexual passion and turns to cold-hearted, detached rape. Alejo, by contrast, is impotent and claims to be devoid of feelings. The entire play contains only brief moments when one character actually relates to another one: One is in scene 2 as Leticia confides to Alejo her dream of becoming educated and her disappointment in her marriage; another is the brief patty-cake game between Olimpia and Nena at the beginning of scene 11. In a sustained encounter, Nena tells Olimpia her story in scene 15. Otherwise, characters seem either to pass one another by or abuse one another.

Of the five characters, Orlando stands at the center of the spectacle. It is his progressive estrangement from others, and ultimately from himself, that constitutes the essential action of the play. He starts the play all by himself. Dressed in military britches, held up by suspenders, and his riding boots, he is in a dark corner of the dining room doing jumping jacks "as long as it can be endured." When he finally stops and wipes the perspiration from his face, he talks to himself, urging himself to do whatever needs to be done "to achieve maximum power." He determines that he will gain promotion from his present rank as lieutenant and move on to higher levels. Leticia cannot be an obstacle to his advancement, and he will marry a woman of high station if need be. Above all, he tells himself, he must put aside sexual passion or "I will be degraded beyond hope of discovery." In scene 2, he has already attained the rank of lieutenant commander, and now he mocks Leticia's resistance to the hunting and killing of innocent creatures as well as her notion of giving money to the poor. In the very next scene, he has found a perverse way to control his sexual passion: He kidnaps and rapes a young girl whom he keeps in the warehouse for his continued convenience. Sex has become something apart from himself, something hidden, and so need not be dealt with. It will not interfere with his ambitions. The most graphic expression of this detachment comes with his description in scene 6 of a stallion mounting a mare:

> He made loud sounds not high-pitched like a horse. He sounded like a whale, like a wounded whale. He was pouring liquid from everywhere, his mouth, his nose, his eyes. He was not a horse but a sexual organ—Helpless. A viscera—Screaming. Making strange sounds. He collapsed on top of her. She wanted him off but he collapsed on top of her and stayed there on top of her. Like gum. He looked more like a whale than a horse. A seal. His muscles were soft. What does it feel like to be without shape like that. Without pride. She was indifferent. He stayed there for a while and then lifted himself off her and to the ground. *(Pause.)* He looked like a horse again.

This story, which he tells to Alejo, is fascinating to him. We might surmise that its interest derives from its parallel to his own detached and dehumanized conduct of sexual life. That attitude takes another disturbing turn at the end of the scene. Alejo announces that he has come to know what viciousness is:

ORLANDO: What is viciousness?

ALEJO: You.

ORLANDO: Me?

ALEJO: The way you tortured Felo.

ORLANDO: I never tortured Felo.

ALEJO: You did.

ORLANDO: Boys play that way. You did too.

ALEJO: I didn't.

ORLANDO: He was repulsive to us.

ALEJO: I never hurt him.

ORLANDO: Well, you never stopped me.

ALEJO: I didn't know how to stop you. I didn't know anyone could behave the way you did. It frightened me. It changed me. I became hopeless. . . .

ORLANDO: You were always hopeless.

After Orlando has left, Alejo turns to Leticia and asks, "How can one live in a world that festers the way ours does and take any pleasure in life?"

Orlando's work in the new department as interrogator leads him to killing the people he interrogates, and by scene 10 he is in trouble for it. He has become too blatant and is now embarrassing his supervisors, Antonio and Velez, as well as the government itself. He becomes depressed. By the end of the scene, he has turned in on himself, talking to himself about how fragile people are that they can die if you just touch them. This state of mind makes him aggressive in the next scene (11) as he verbally attacks first Nena and then Olimpia. Scene 13 is devoted to a monologue

Orlando delivers to Nena, perhaps the only time in the course of the play that Orlando makes an honest statement about his confused and alienated self:

> What I do to you is out of love. Out of want. It's not what you think. I wish you didn't have to be hurt. I don't do it out of hatred. It is not out of rage. It is love. It is a quiet feeling. It's a pleasure. It is quiet and it pierces my insides in the most internal way. It is my most private self. And this I give to you.— Don't be afraid.—It is a desire to destroy and to see things destroyed and to see the inside of them.—It's my nature. I must hide this from others. But I don't feel remorse. I was born this way and I must have this.—I need love. I wish you did not feel hurt and recoil from me.

From this point, starting with scene 14 and carrying through scene 17, attention shifts to the effect Orlando's transformation has on the women of the house. Leticia has discovered Nena in the house and what Orlando is doing to her. First she protests and wants her out of the house, then she asks him not to make Nena scream, and then she wants Mona to come live here and support her. Orlando denies her all of these requests and informs her that Nena will be elevated to a servant in the house. Scene 15 is a sustained interchange between Olimpia and Nena, who tells her story of her lost grandfather and of being beaten by Orlando, something he must do, she says, because she is dirty: "The dirt won't go away from inside me." In the next scene (16), Leticia speaks at length to Mona by telephone about the horror she feels at Orlando's violent life. Finally, Olimpia in scene 17 becomes absorbed in the little things that irritate—high-heeled shoes, ingrown toenails, sugar in the blood—as a way of avoiding her circumstance.

The play comes to a rapid close with the last two scenes, and Orlando's viciousness literally comes home. He is being attacked in his nightmare in scene 18, and he awakens to a telephone call that seems to confirm his suspicion that Leticia has taken a lover. He then sets up an interrogation for the final scene, seating Leticia in a chair facing forward, barking questions at her, pulling her hair, and forcing her confession about arranging a rendezvous with Albertico Estevez. The play ends quickly. He puts his hand in her blouse, we hear her excruciating scream, he walks away, and she shoots him.

The final moment, Leticia putting the gun in Nena's hand and saying "Please . . . ," could mean any number of things, as mentioned earlier. She offers the gun because Nena may well need it at some point in her life. Or she may be requesting that Nena shoot her as punishment for her crime. She may be asking that Nena take the blame for the murder. Or the request may be for something quite different. The lights fade and we do not know. The very ambiguity of this final moment grows naturally out of the violent and inhumane world that surrounds the household, creating an atmosphere that squelches all genuine humanity in women as well as in men.

What we have witnessed in the quick succession of nineteen scenes leaves us with swirling images of a viciousness that pervades the whole of the outside world. And it invades the inner domestic world. In doing so, it empties everyone, both the perpetrators of sexual and political violence and their victims, of any form of shared humanity. The play is certainly not an attack on South American politics per se. No reference is ever made to the specific time or place of the action. Instead, it draws on the skewed, patriarchal system generally associated with such societies. The politics of corruption, vaunting power, domination, violence, and oppression can all too readily emerge in a male-dominated society, not because men are inherently bad but because it creates a dangerous imbalance in the social order. When that happens, everyone suffers, both men and women. This is a feminist stance, certainly, a feminism that argues for a better world. As Alejo says, "How can one live in a world that festers the way ours does and take any pleasure in life?"

APPENDIX D

Bibliography

A List of Books Relevant to Script Analysis

Ball, David. *Backwards and Forwards.* Carbondale: Southern Illinois University Press, 1983.
Ball develops an approach to script analysis that explores how factors accumulate in the forward movement of the script and are clarified by looking at that movement backward.

Beckerman, Bernard. *The Dynamics of Drama.* New York: Drama Book Publishers, 1979.
This is a comprehensive and thorough examination of dramatic elements and how they contribute to a play's effects. Beckerman offers a "vertical analysis" assessing how elements come together to produce major moments in the course of a play.

Brockett, Oscar. *The Theatre: An Introduction.* New York: Holt, Rinehart and Winston, 1974.
Brockett includes a full chapter on "Dramatic Structure, Form and Style" and provides thorough analyses of many plays from Greek times to the present. This material also appears in his brief version of this book, *The Essential Theatre.*

Castagno, Paul. *New Playwriting Strategies.* New York: Routledge, 2001.
Castagno explores approaches to playwriting that entail very different structures from those traditionally held as standard. He sees these new strategies as "multi-vocal" in Bakhtin's sense of the word, and he relies on the work of playwrights Len Jenkin, Eric Overmyer, and Max Wellman.

Gross, Roger. *Understanding Play Scripts: Theory and Method.* Bowling Green, WI: Bowling Green University Press, 1974.
Gross lays out a theoretical foundation for a process of script analysis. Much of the book is devoted to questions of interpretation: What are its limits and challenges?

Grote, David. *Script Analysis: Reading and Understanding the Playscript for Production.* Belmont, CA: Wadsworth, 1985.
The approach taken by Grote is based on three components: a chronology of the play's action, the characters, and the audience. The book ends with ways of arriving at a synthesis.

Hayman, Ronald. *How to Read a Play.* New York: Grove Press, 1977.
This book is addressed to the reader interested in the act of reading play scripts and understanding the implications inherent in them for staging.

Hodge, Francis. *Play Directing: Analysis, Communication and Style.* Englewood Cliffs, NJ: Prentice-Hall, 1982.
This is a text on directing but based on the conviction that analysis must serve as its basis. Accordingly, Hodge devotes a substantial section to the process of script analysis.

Hornby, Roger. *Script into Performance: A Structuralist View of Play Production.* Austin: University of Texas Press, 1977.
Hornby emphasizes the structure of action inherent in a script with an eye to its realization in performance.

Ingham, Rosemary. *From the Page to the Stage: How Theatre Designers Make Connections between Scripts and Images.* Portsmouth, NH: Heinemann, 1998
Ingham presents a designer's approach to the study of a script, detailing the processes of analysis, imagination, and research that go into the realization of set, costume, and lighting design.

Price, Thomas. *Dramatic Structure and Meaning in Theatrical Productions.* San Francisco: EMText, 1992.
Based on a dialectical approach to dramatic structure, this book postulates that there are seven basic movement patterns in drama. The study proceeds from theorem to theorem building the case and then illustrates with analyses of scripts that conform to each pattern.

Scanlon, David. *Reading Drama.* Mountain View, CA: Mayfield, 1988.
Scanlon approaches scripts from a historical orientation. He addresses dramatic principles and illustrates how they alter from one historical period to another. His book deals with such matters as genre, the fictional world, characterization, and structure.

States, Bert O. *Great Reckonings in Little Rooms.* Berkeley: University of California Press, 1985.
States explores theatre art as experience and accordingly takes a phenomenological approach. He builds a case against semiotics on the ground that it reduces theatre to a vehicle for signs, and overlooks its sensory and immediate experience.

Styan, J. L. *Drama, Stage and Audience.* London: Cambridge University Press, 1975.
Based on an Aristotelian approach, Styan explores the relationship between script, theatrical production, and the audience. He uses sustained examples of analysis of scripts.

Styan, J. L. *Elements of the Drama.* Cambridge: Cambridge University Press, 1960.
Similar to Styan's later book, this investigates the elements of the drama defined in Aristotle's terms and then applies them to a series of specific scripts.

Thomas, James. *Playscript Analysis for Actors, Directors, and Designers.* Boston: Focal Press, 1999.
This is an approach to the work theatre artists must undertake in investigating the implications of the script as they work on its production. The analysis breaks down the script in terms of Aristotle's six elements.

Waxberg, Charles. *The Actor's Script: Script Analysis for Performers.* Portsmouth, NH: Heineman, 1999.
Waxberg provides ways for the actor to explore character by breaking down the script into character objectives, motivations, obstacles, and beats.

Weales, Gerald. *A Play and Its Parts.* New York: Basic Books, 1964.
The book proceeds from the conviction that the important distinction of drama from other forms of literature is performance. It explores the parts of a play in terms of action, language, gesture, sets and props, lights and sound, costume, and stage space and ends with a chapter on meaning.

Whitman, Robert F. *The Play-Reader's Handbook.* Indianapolis, IN: Bobbs-Merrill, 1966.
This is an investigation of drama in terms of its relation to reality. It is structured in two parts, the first having to do with how "reality" operates in the drama and the second with how views of reality are reflected in the plays of significant periods in history.

INDEX